GODS, BEASTS AND MEN

A Book of Greek Stories

JO MANTON

Illustrated by
Dorothy Ralphs

HULTON EDUCATIONAL PUBLICATIONS

© *J. Manton 1974*

ISBN 0 7175 0662 2

YH012608

First published 1974 by
Hulton Educational Publications Ltd.,
Raans Road, Amersham, Bucks.
Printed in Great Britain by Tinling (1973) Ltd.,
Prescot and London.

LIST OF NAMES

vii

Greek names are easy to pronounce if you follow these simple rules: C is pronounced *k*, ch is *kh*, g is always hard as in *go*, ph is *f* as in *ph*one, eu is always *you*. Diphthongs are long, likewise vowels with the sign (-) above them as ō which is pronounced *oh*.

The accent is marked with the symbol (').

A-ché-lō-us
A-chíl-lēs
A-coé-tēs
Ā-crí-si-us
Ae-é-tes
Aé-geus
Aé-o-lus
Aé-thra
Alc-mé-na
Á-ma-zon (*English pronunciation*)*
Am-phí-try-ōn
An-dró-ma-chē
An-dró-me-da
A-phro-dí-tē
A-pól-lō
Ar-cá-di-a (*English pronunciation*)
Árēs
Ár-gō
Ár-go-naut
Ár-gos
A-ri-ád-nē
A-rí-ōn
Ár-te-mis ·
As-clé-pi-us
A-ta-lán-ta
Áth-a-mas
A-thé-na
Át-las
Au-gé-as

Báu-cis
Bel-lé-ro-phōn
Bós-pho-rus
Cád-mus
Cá-ly-dōn
Cal-lýp-sō
Cás-tor
Cén-taur
Cé-pha-lus
Cér-be-rus
Cér-cy-on
Chá-ron (*English pronunciation*)
Chí-ron
Chí-máe-ra
Cīr-cē
Cnōs-sos
Col-chis
Crēte
Cró-nus
Cy-a-nē
Cý-clops
Cý-clopes (pluval)
Dáe-da-lus
Da ná-ē
Dá-na-us
Dei-a-ní-ra
Dé-los
Dél-phī
Dē-mē-ter
Díc-tē

List of Names

Dē-mḗ-ter
Díc-tē
Díc-tys
Di-o-nȳ́-sus
Drȳ́-ad (*English pronunciation*)
É-chō (*English pronunciation*)
É-lys
Ē-lȳ́-si-um
É-ós
E-pi-mḗ-theus
E-ry-mán-theus
Eu-rṓ-pa
Eu-rȳ́-di-cē
Eu-rȳ́s-theus
Gór-gon
Hā́-dēs
Hé-ca-tē
Héc-tor
Hé-cu-ba
Hél-lē
Hél-les-pont (*English pronunciation*)
Hé-li-con (*English pronunciation*)
Hḗ-li-os
He-pháe-stus
Hḗ-ra
Hḗ-ra-clēs
Hér-mēs
Hes-pé-ri-dēs
Hés-ti-a
Hip-pó-ly-ta
Hȳ́-dra
Hȳ́-las (*English pronunciation*)
Ī́-da
I-ó-ba-tēs
Í-o-lus
Í-phi-clēs
Í-ris
Í-tha-ca
Jā́-son (*English pronunciation*)
La-ó-co-on (*English pronunciation*)
Lḗ-da
Lḗto
Lȳ́-ci-a
Lȳ́n-ceus
Mē-dḗ-a
Me-dū́-sa
Me-le-ā́-ger
Me-ne-lā́-us
Mī́-das (*English pronunciation*)
Mī-lá-niōn
Mī́-nō-taur
Móp-sus
Mȳ-cḗ-nae (*English pronunciation*)
Náx-os
Ne-mé-a
Né-phe-lē
Nḗ-rē-id
Nés-sus
Nȳ́-sa
O-dȳ́s-seus
O-lȳ́m-pus
Ór-pheus
Ō-rī́-on (*English pronunciation*)
Pan-dṓ-ra
Pa-trō-clus
Pé-ga-sus (*English pronunciation*)
Pé-li-as
Pḗ-leus
Pé-lops
Per-sé-pho-nē
Pér-seus

List of Names

Phi-lḗ-mon
Phí-neus
Phríx-us
Pleí-a-des
Po-ly-déu-cēs
Po-ly-phḗ-mus
Po-seī-don (*English pronunciation*)
Prī-am (*English pronunciation*)
Pró-cris
Pro-mḗ-theus
Psȳ́-chē
Pȳ́-thi-a
Rhé-a
Sá-tyr
Scȳ́-thi-a
Scy-ros
Sé-ri-phus
Sī-lḗ-nus
Sī-nis
Sī-ren (*English pronunciation*)
Sí-sy-phus
Stym-phā́-lus
Stýx
Tán-ta-lus
Tár-tar-us
Thḗ-seus
Thḗ-tis
Thrắce
Tī́-phys
Tí-ryns
Tī́-tan
Tróe-zēn
Zeús
Zṓ-di-ac

*Where the Greek and English syllabic quantities are at variance the standard English pronunciation has been followed.

Note Almost all the names used in these stories are in the Greek form. However the Latin form occurs occasionally, e.g. 'Cupid' (Greek 'Eros') when the source is a Latin author.

CONTENTS

(Sources of stories in brackets)

	Page
THE TELLING OF TALES	12
THE BIRTH OF GODS, BEASTS AND MEN	15
The Birth of the Gods	17
The Coming of Fire	22
The God's Revenge (Hesiod, *Theogony* and *Works and Days*)	26
WORLD AND UNDERWORLD	31
The Stealing of Persephone (*Homeric Hymn to Demeter*)	33
Orpheus in the Underworld (Virgil, *Georgics*)	39
HEROES AND MONSTERS	45
Perseus in the Chest	47
Perseus slays the Gorgon	51
Perseus and the Sea-Monster (Ovid, *Metamorphoses*)	57
Heracles the Young Hero	62
The Labours of Heracles I and II	66, 73
Heracles on Olympus (Apollodorus, *Bibliotheca*)	79
STRANGE JOURNEYS	85
The Girl on the Bull (Moschus, *Idylls*)	87
The Winged Horse (Pindar, *Olympian Odes*)	90
The Man on a Dolphin (Ovid, *Metamorphoses*)	95
The Flying Ram (Apollonius Rhodius, *Argonautica*)	99

	Page
Two Heroes who were Mortals	105
The Man with one Understanding	107
The Voyage of the 'Argo'	113
Jason wins the Golden Fleece (Apollonius Rhodius, *Argonautica*)	120
Theseus and the Bandits	126
Theseus slays the Minotaur	132
King Theseus (Plutarch, *Lives*)	138
Love and Magic	143
Three Golden Apples (Apollodorus, *Bibliotheca*)	145
The Hunter and the Nymph (Ovid, *Metamorphoses*)	150
The Tasks of Psyche (Apuleius, *The Golden Ass*)	154
Greeks and Trojans	161
Achilles kills Hector	163
The Wooden Horse of Troy	170
The Cyclops' Cave	175
The Enchantress's Palace (Homer, *Iliad* and *Odyssey*)	180
Strange Shapes	187
The Pirate Ship (*Homeric Hymn to Dionysus*)	189
King Midas	194
The Country Cottage	200
The Spirits of Wild Places (Ovid, *Metamorphoses*)	205
The Tellers of Tales	211

The Telling of Tales

"ALL men honour the tellers of tales," said the Greeks, for they hold man's life in memory, like water in a cup. The earliest farmers and keepers of the hearth fire lived by the changing seasons, by sun and moon, rain, wind and clouds. Slowly in their minds the powers of nature took the shape of unknown beings, to be worshipped and appeased. Their rituals ran through all life. "Never cross a stream," said an early farmer, "without gazing into its depths, washing in its pure water and praying." A pool among dry rocks, where beasts could drink, came to these people like the gift of some unknown friend. A thunderstorm which flattened the standing barley came like the curse of some mighty enemy. They sacrificed to the sun and moon, to earth, air and fire. After the worship of earth, which gives life and food, came the worship of heaven. Slowly the fertility magic of country places grew into the mystery of the gods.

The gods and goddesses lived, higher than clouds or eagles on the wing, in a shining palace on Mount Olympus. They drew breath like men, loved, hated and fought like men; but all men die and the gods live for ever. Their huge battles with giants and Titans made flood, fire and earthquake in the land of men. Their anger was death itself. Each had his sacred beast whose nature he shared: Zeus the potent bull, Athena the far-seeing owl, Artemis the wild bear, and Aphrodite, the amorous dove. The gods were alive with the life-blood of all living things, entwined in the leaves, crouched in the beasts, soaring with the eagle or wearing the many faces of men to work their will. Behind them, unseen, lived the shadowy powers of nature from which they had come. Their tales were life itself.

Old men told tales of the gods on windy nights, as they sat wrapped in their cloaks round the fire. Women sang them, spinning on their doorsteps at evening or walking to and fro at the loom. Parents told them to children as shining example or black threat. Blind men led by boys, like the street musicians still seen in Greece, travelled from city to city, telling tales of gods and heroes, of the birth of the world, of exploration, cunning tricks and strange shapes.

People listened to these tales to learn the cause and meaning of all things: how the earth and stars were created or water divided from dry land, how their own cities were founded, why some people seem by nature brave and generous, others small-minded and mean. In the wayward family of gods and goddesses, living idly at home, often quarrelling, looking down through the clouds on men, or visiting earth for their pleasure, they took delight in recognizing people like themselves. So all house doors were flung open to welcome the tellers of tales. Their fame travelled from city to city and from one century to another. These are some of the tales they told.

The Birth of Gods, Beasts and Men

The Birth of the Gods

AT the beginning of all things was a great emptiness filled with whirling atoms. Out of these grew Earth, mother of all gods, beasts and men, with the starry sky above her and the dark caverns of the underworld beneath. Rain fell from the sky on the bare hills and deep clefts of earth and from this first marriage of earth and heaven came every living thing: grass and water, trees, green plants and the deep, swirling sea. The first children Earth bore were monsters, three Giants, each with a hundred hands, and three Cyclopes, each with one staring eye in the middle of his forehead.

The next brood were the Titans, huge, terrible children. Their father, the sky, hated these monstrous sons from the first and forced them back into the body of earth, pressing heavy mountains down upon them. But the Titans were forces of nature, and fought for their freedom with all nature's weapons. They hurled grinding ice, dark floods to cover the land, fountains of pure volcanic fire, molten rivers roaring as they poured down the mountain sides. All creation groaned as nature warred with itself.

The Titans hacked their father's body with sickles of jagged flint and cast him down into the shadowy underworld. His blood fell on earth, where the avenging Furies, who punish murder, sprang up out of the soil. Other drops fell into the sea. There the white surge brought forth the first goddess, naked Aphrodite. She rose from the foam; soft winds wafted her to land and wherever she set her foot grass and flowers sprang up, for she was the bringer of desire and fertility, which creates all things.

Aphrodite of the sudden glances was the first and last of goddesses, who still has power over the minds of men. Earth also bore Night, and Night's dark family of children, mysterious sleep with all his family of dreams and the three Fates which give men good or evil fortunes. Last, Night bore Death. These things, desire, sleep, fate and death make up the life of man. From the beginning of the world until now no man or woman living has escaped them, nor ever will.

Now sky was banished and Cronus, the wily, terrible youngest of the Titans ruled creation in his father's place. He cast down his savage brothers the Giants and Cyclopes into the depths of earth where they raged and roared through fiery mouths. His brother Titans he left on earth, for nature needed their huge powers. They were the sun, the moon, the rosy dawn, the stars and Atlas, who holds up the curving sky on his broad shoulders. The wisest of all Titans, Prometheus, went to live on earth, watching patiently over the slow birth of the first reptiles, birds and beasts.

Cronus did not guess these creatures of earth might one day overthrow him, for like all tyrants he feared danger nearer at hand. His dying father put a curse on him, as he fell from the sky. "You cast me down and killed me; your sons will do the same to you." So Cronus watched in fear.

He married a sister-Titan, Rhea the mistress of the lions, who bore him children: first, three daughters—Hestia, bright-haired Demeter and Hera of the golden sandals, then two sons—Poseidon and dark Hades. Every year as these children were born, Cronus remembered his father's curse and devoured them whole.

Rhea was enraged, and determined to save her next son, Zeus. She bore him in blackest night and gave him to her own

The Birth of the Gods

mother, Earth, to hide. Then she wrapped a large stone in swaddling clothes and showed it to Cronus, who seized it with both huge hands and swallowed it whole, convinced it was another child. But the real Zeus was hidden in the secret depths of a cave in the mountains; two nymphs, the spirits of this wild place, cared for him. They fed him with honey from their bees and milk from their goat, which he shared with his shaggy half-brother, goat-footed Pan. His cradle rocked in a tree, so that Cronus could not find him either in air or earth. Armed Titans clashed their spears against their shields to drown his crying, so that Cronus could not hear it from his haunted throne. The child Zeus grew strong and glorious and returned at last to the house of his parents, seeking revenge.

Rhea, who still mourned her lost children, helped Zeus. She made him cup-bearer at his father's feasts and gave him potent herbs to mix with the honeyed drink, drugs strong enough to turn a giant's stomach. Cronus took the cup, drank deep and staggered. With groans and heaves, mighty as earthquakes, he vomited out, first the great stone, then the living full-grown brothers and sisters of Zeus. The stone you may still see, for it has lain at Delphi in the heart of Greece from that day to this; the Greeks called it "the navel of the earth"

Then the wronged brothers and sisters made war on their terrible father, as the curse had foretold. The war raged ten years but neither side could win, though the earth was torn apart and blackened with battle. At last the aging Cronus asked advice from Prometheus, the wise Titan, who answered, "Bring up your brothers from the underworld." But Cronus was afraid of his savage brothers with the one eye, or the hundred hands, and he refused. Then Prometheus gave the same advice to Zeus, who was wise enough to listen.

Zeus took the key of bronze and went down into the underworld; nine days and nights a stone would fall before it came to that dark place. Zeus turned the mighty key in the lock with a crash that shook the world; Giants and Cyclopes, the monsters of our earliest history, poured out upon the quaking earth. Zeus feasted them with the food and drink of the gods, dangerous because it gave them immortality. Then he held a council of war with his terrible allies, shouting, "Now we will fight and win!" The Cyclopes hammered weapons in their roaring volcano forge: for Poseidon a three-pronged spear, for Hades a helmet of invisibility and for Zeus the thunderbolt against which nothing can stand.

The rebel sons made their plan. Hades put on the helmet and crept upon Cronus unseen, stealing his weapons. Poseidon brandished the trident to distract his attention and Zeus struck him down with a thunderbolt. Then Zeus the Thunderer fought the army of his father Cronus in mid-air. Ever after, men told stories of the thunderstorm which was that battle. There was a terrible cry from the boundless sea, a shattering of the earth; the broad sky groaned and the forest burst into flames as Zeus hurled his thunderbolts.

The giants threw rocks and hailstones with their hundred hands, and Pan, horned and wild-eyed, gave the loudest shout ever heard. The army of Cronus fled in the utter fear men still call panic. So the gods, who were children of heaven, defeated the Titans who were children of earth. Zeus buried them deep in earth, where red flame rolls, pressing down mountains on their shaggy chests. Zeus and his brothers might have fought each other but wise Prometheus advised them to draw lots from the helmet for their kingdoms. Poseidon became lord of the restless, unharvested sea, and Hades of the dark under- world. Zeus became ruler of the sky, and the worship of mother Earth, who gives life, gave way to the worship of heaven.

Next Zeus gave to each of his sisters her work and her kingdom. Aphrodite already had power over the hearts of gods and men alike; even the beasts fawned on her and she sent them off in couples to the shadowy dells, to return bringing their cubs. Hestia became keeper of the hearth fire, the sacred centre of every home. Bright-haired Demeter he made corn queen and apple-bearer, who gives men joy in their harvests. Hera, whose name means the Year, he married; in spring a girl, in summer a wife, in autumn a widow, she is all women.

These six sons and daughters of Cronus were the older gods; the younger were children of Zeus. Athena sprang from his head, full-grown and armed in glittering gold. She brought wisdom and skill to all who would hear her. By Hera he had two sons, Ares the god of war, and Hephaestus the lame blacksmith god. By a nymph he had Hermes, a child so clever that he was born in the morning, played the harp at mid-day and stole cattle in the evening. Zeus gave him winged sandals and a herald's staff and made him messenger of the gods. Another nymph bore him twins, golden Apollo who ruled the sun and his silver sister Artemis. These twelve made up the family of the immortals who lived on Olympus's shining floor.

Beyond them, Zeus had countless children. His wife was jealous and watchful, but he escaped her by a hundred disguises. Ageless, powerful, he twisted into bull, ram, serpent or golden rain to capture a goddess, a nymph or a girl. He begot tall heroes, monsters, gods, whose tale is still told. He is the thrower of thunderbolts, giver of rain and dew to the thirsty land. He can catch the winged eagle in the air and outswim the dolphin in the sea, and break the proud spirit of man. For Zeus who fought and conquered the forces of nature is the ruler of all things.

The Coming of Fire

THERE came a time when Earth had made living things of all kinds, beasts, birds, fishes and grasses; but there were still no men. By strength and cunning Zeus had overpowered his father. He alone held the white fire of lightning and sent his thunder ringing round the sky. He was king of the gods but there were no men for him to rule. Then Earth said, "I will be the mother not only of plants which cannot feel, or beasts which cannot think, but also of reasoning creatures." So, out of water, earth and fire she slowly formed the first stumbling human creatures, who lifted bewildered faces to the sky. They were children of earth but also children of heaven. It is woman who imitates Earth when she bears a child, not Earth who imitates woman. These first men Earth bore married the first women and their children formed primitive tribes. They were called people.

Zeus remembered that two Titans, Prometheus and his brother Epimetheus, lived on earth and knew the powers of nature. So he commanded them, "Give to all living creatures the gifts they need to survive." The two brothers were as different as their names. Prometheus, whose name means forethought, reasoned all things out before he acted. Epimetheus, whose name means afterthought, acted first and learnt by his mistakes afterwards. So now each acted according to his nature.

Epimetheus rushed impulsively over earth with his great Titan's tread, giving all beauties, senses and powers to the wild beasts. He gave courage to the lion, strength to the bull, cunning to the fox, keen sight to the eagle, rich fur to the bear, speed and matchless beauty to the dappled deer. Nothing was left over for the people. Prometheus breathed life into their lumpish bodies, but that was all. They were poor, naked, two-legged animals, without knowledge to feed or clothe themselves. They crouched in the plain, eating wild grass, or huddled in caves to shelter from winter's driving sleet.

When Zeus looked down from Olympus and saw the people, he thought them poor brutes; he would have liked to destroy them and make something finer to live with the glorious beasts and trees of earth. Secretly he resented the power of thought within their ugly skulls. He could work his will with sky and clouds, mountains and forests; thinking men, however, might one day defy him. He made ready to hurl a thunderbolt. But Prometheus defended his people. He felt a bond with men for he had watched over their birth and he suffered or was glad with them.

Patiently the wise Titan went to work, generation by generation, to teach the people all the hard things they must learn: how to tame dog and horse, how to plough with a bent stick, how to sow seeds in spring and find berries at fall of leaf. He taught them to sacrifice to the gods, but to keep the best part of the offering for themselves and burn only the dry bones on the altar. Zeus was a jealous god, and this was the worst of insults. Rage smouldered in his heart; he swore he would think out calamities for man, and all of them came to pass.

First he determined to hide fire from the miserable mortals who shuddered peltless in frost and rain. So Zeus kept fire for the gods in his sacred hearth on Olympus, or in Hephaestus's roaring forge. Men did not know fire existed; but Prometheus knew. Also he loved to match his wits against Zeus. So, with deep thought, he found a way to cheat the king of the gods and give the people forbidden fire.

As a Titan Prometheus was free to visit the gods in their sky palace, hidden by clouds from the eyes of men. Prometheus took a tall plant of fennel, which has a hollow stalk. He trimmed the leaves, slit one end of the stalk and carried it to heaven disguised as a walking staff. When he was alone on the immense shining floor above Olympus, he stole a smouldering twig from the hearth of Zeus. Then with the fire from heaven hidden in his hollow staff, he strode calmly down Mount Olympus to the home of mankind. There he lit the first fire on earth. The people crept close and crouched around the flickering, live thing in wonder. Men and women stretched rough, hairy hands to the blaze and saw the flames shine in each other's eyes. Healing warmth spread through their numbed bodies. When Zeus saw this, rage devoured his heart to the depths. "You are happy, O subtle Prometheus," he said, "because you cheated me and stole fire. But it will be a disaster to you and to all the race of men for ever." So saying, the father of the gods laughed bitterly, he had already imagined a sweet revenge.

For Prometheus, who had outwitted him, Zeus made a cruel torture. He ordered Hephaestus to bind the Titan in chains of knotted bronze and carry him to the highest peak of the freezing Caucasus mountains. There Zeus drove an arrow through Prometheus's body, nailing him to the icy crags. Each day Zeus sent an eagle to devour his living flesh with iron beak and talons, but each night the wounds healed to prolong his agony. So Prometheus lay bound for thirteen generations, forced to bear the anger of Zeus.

Beasts suffer dumbly without understanding, but man has the mind to rebel. As men grew slowly wiser they began to question why Prometheus should suffer so. They imagined him bound to his crag among the shrieking storms and saying, "This shame, these chains are put on me by the new ruler of the gods. O earth, O air and sun, behold how I am wronged! The reason is that I loved men too well." Men feared the power of Zeus, but in their secret hearts they blamed him. So from

The Coming of Fire

Prometheus came man's first thoughts of justice and injustice, of right and wrong.

When he brought fire, Prometheus began man's history. The people lit camp fires to scare wild beasts and keep themselves warm. By slow stages they learnt to cook, to fire clay pots, to bake clay bricks and to smelt metal from the rocks. With the secret craft of fire they forged bronze swords and shields. In making and doing they learnt to think for themselves. On the anvil of the blacksmith they forged at last the iron tongue of truth. Hidden in those first flickering fires within the cave were ships on the sea, horse-drawn chariots, the struggle of battle, the hushed theatre, wise laws and the physician's healing touch. The Greeks understood this and ever after the first divine spark, held fire a holy thing. The hearth was a shrine in every household. A girl who married never failed to bring a burning brand from her parents' hearth to kindle the first fire in her new home.

After long ages the hero Heracles, born of Zeus and a mortal woman, unbound Prometheus from his chains. He persuaded his father to relent at last and receive the wise Titan into the company of the immortals. But men did not forget his sufferings and honoured Prometheus who brought the seed of fire from heaven.

The God's Revenge

LOOKING down through the clouds on men, Zeus saw sparks rising from their camp fires on the dark plain, and grudged them their happiness. They sat talking freely, knowing forbidden things yet unafraid. For in his love of men Prometheus, before Zeus bound him, had protected them. He gathered all the troubles of mortal life together and put them in an earthenware jar, tall as a man, with a heavy lid. This he put in the storeroom of his brother Epimetheus. "Take care," he warned. "Never lift the jar's lid, or try to look inside. Above all, never accept any gift from Zeus the Thunderer, for he is man's enemy." Epimetheus, without thinking, promised both these things. Now men were happy, for they lived in a Golden Age free from sickness, pain or fear. These earliest men ate wild fruit and honey, drank wild goats' milk, laughed and danced in the daytime, slept under the stars at night. They had no foreknowledge of the future or of troubles to come. Even death was not terrible to them. They lay down as simply as though they were going to sleep. These happy creatures had neither need nor fear of the gods.

The God's Revenge

Then Zeus swore to make an evil thing for man as the price of fire. He commanded the craftsman god Hephaestus to take a lump of clay from earth and model a shy, gentle-looking girl. Then Athena, mistress of weavers, made her a dress of silver gauze and spread a bridal veil over her meekly-bowed head. The Graces crowned her with flowers. Aphrodite decked her with garlands and perfumed her with the herbs that bring desire. Hermes, the messenger, taught her to speak and behave prettily, but to hide her real thoughts. Then Zeus led her out triumphantly, delighting in the charming trap he had made for men, the first civilized woman. The gods applauded when they saw her, declaring no god could resist her, much less simple man. Zeus named her Pandora, which means all gifts, for each of the gods had given her some special beauty or grace.

Zeus ordered Hermes of the winged sandals to lead Pandora down to earth and offer her as a gift to Epimetheus. He chose this brother for two good reasons: first he had the jar and second he was a fool. So Hermes led Pandora by the hand, and said with winning charm, "This is Pandora. I bring her as a gift from Zeus, to be your wife." At the sight of the fresh, pretty creature Epimetheus forgot, as Zeus had known he would, all the warnings of his wise brother. Though Prometheus had told him any gift from Zeus would be dangerous, he eagerly took this one.

At first he was delighted with his bride. Pandora was submissive and delicious, finding endless ways to please and amuse her husband. But she was new to the earth and, like a puppy or any young growing creature, endlessly curious about each new discovery. She followed Epimetheus everywhere, watching him with innocent round eyes. She saw that he never touched a certain tall jar, which always stood in its place at the back of the courtyard; dust was beginning to gather on it. "What is in that jar, my husband?" she asked in her small, beguiling voice. "Never mind!" answered Epimetheus, lordly as befits a husband. "Very well, dear husband," whispered Pandora in her little girl's voice, and he was such a fool that not even this meekness made him suspicious.

Of course Pandora only waited until Epimetheus went out

hunting to run straight to the back of the courtyard. Standing on tiptoe, she stretched up her small, soft hands to the jar, and lifted the heavy lid. Like a rushing wind, out flew plague and famine, war and sudden death, murder, envy, hatred, madness, hard labour and weary old age. Pandora cried out in childish fright and let the stone lid fall back, trapping hope, which still lay in the depths of the jar. But it was too late to prevent calamity. Husband and wife, with all the race of mortals after them, were attacked by all the ills of the flesh. Zeus had his revenge.

From the first there were some who called this tale of a jar nonsense. What Zeus sent to punish man, they said, was woman herself, foolish, frivolous and lazy. Men are the bees who work all day to fill the honeycomb, women the idle drones who stay in the hive and eat up all the honey. No one can alter them, for Zeus has made them so. Naturally women deny this. Pandora, they say, came out of earth, bringing food and children as woman's gifts; her jar contained the fruits of the earth. Troubles come because man does not use these wisely. Men and women have argued about this ever since. Whatever the truth, after Pandora opened the jar the Golden Age ended and a Silver Age followed. Men were like children; living only a short time, they wasted their lives in foolish quarrels and died without understanding the meaning of things.

Next came a Bronze Age of men who loved war. These were the heroes who slew monsters, found the golden fleece and captured Troy. Their tales are still told. Last came the Age of Iron. Even parents and children no longer loved one another truly and might was right. Those were bad days to live through.

Once the Golden Age was ended, men could no longer live without toil. They were forced to strip their bodies to plough and sow, begging Demeter to grant them good harvests. They learnt by hard necessity all the lore of the countryside. Harvest begins when the Pleiades rise in the sky, and ploughing when they sink. Store your hay and corn and keep a fierce watchdog to frighten away robbers. Autumn rain follows and the leaves fall; then is the time to cut your firewood. The winter cry of the heron in the clouds tells you to go to your fields and plough a straight furrow. When the swallow comes one morning, spring is here; get up at once and prune your vines. The slug crawls out to eat the young green plants; that shows it is time to sharpen your fag-hooks. Every season brings hard labour. The best a man can hope for is brief rest: sometimes in winter when the north wind blows to sit beside the fire wearing sheepskin slippers with the fur inside, sometimes in summer when the grasshopper sings all day, to lie in the shade of the rocks with some friends, sharing a jug of wine. These pleasures are soon over. A man could only hope to be happy if he kept all these rules and lived blamelessly before the all-seeing gods.

Worst of the troubles in Pandora's fatal jar was the last trouble of all, the fear of death. From now on men knew that they must die, though the gods live for ever. They sensed the presence of the gods above and around them everywhere, felt it in the forest at mid-day, heard it in the hidden streams. They knew the gods were children of Earth like themselves, like them in form and feeling, yet this great difference held them apart. "We can," said the Greeks, "be great in mind and body like the immortal gods. Yet we can never know the end, by day or in the night, to which our fate has written we will come." Men needed the gods to protect them from the vast dangers of the world, but the gods needed men to honour them with words and ritual offerings. So for their long, many-coloured history they lived in glory or grief, man and gods together.

World and Underworld

The Stealing of Persephone

UNDER the mountain of Etna in Sicily is a lake of deep water. Swans sing there, and green boughs screen the light. There bright-haired Demeter, apple-bearer and corn-queen, left her child Persephone, when she travelled over the earth to give life to the crops in their season. Persephone passed her days with the nymphs picking wild flowers, filling the skirt of her dress with dark violets, crocuses, iris, and the fleshy plant the people of that country call sorcerers' fingers. "Look, Persephone," the nymphs called, pointing to each in turn, and the child ran from one to another, surprised with delight. One day Persephone saw, shining like a star in a dark cleft of the mountain, a flower more beautiful than any she had seen before. Earth had grown it as a trap for this flowerlike girl; such was the will of the gods. Persephone ran towards it, looked back to see if the nymphs were following, then ran on alone. Twisted black rocks closed in around her, and sharp stones cut her feet; but she did not notice them, for the flower was almost within her grasp, a honey-scented narcissus with golden eyes, surely a magic plant. Earth and sky laughed aloud for joy at its beauty, and the child of Earth reached out both hands to pick it.

Suddenly there was a distant roar, deep in the heart of the volcanic mountain, and a crash of falling rocks all around her. "The rocks are falling!" cried Persephone in dread. "The earth is opening under me!" "Persephone," said a voice of terrible quietness, which seemed to come from beneath her feet. The mountain heaved open around her and a chariot pulled by four black horses rose from out of the earth. The horses strained in the traces, their eyes wild and their nostrils streaming flame; the earth rang with the clang of their hooves, but the driver held them with an iron hand.

At the sight of his face, Persephone gave a cry and tried to run for safety, but before she had gone three steps he caught her by her long gold hair. With one swift movement he wrapped her in his black cloak, swept her into the chariot and turned the horses back to the underworld below the earth. "Persephone," he said," I will take you to my country under the earth, where precious metals lie buried and the great trees turn to coal. You shall sit by my side as a queen there, for I am Hades, the King of the Dead."

The nymph Cyane heard and ran to stop him, stretching her arms to bar the way and calling him not to frighten the child. But Hades was a powerful god. At his frown the nymph's body dissolved into her own tears, and where she had been lay a blue lake. You may still see the lonely water, still hear the murmur of her springs like a voice weeping. It is Cyane weeping for her friend. Persephone's cries for help grew fainter as the crater opened and the chariot swept her into the earth. So long as she could see the sun and smell the living land, she cried till the mountain peaks rang. Far away among the vineyards and lemon orchards of the plain Demeter heard with deep-stabbing anguish and knew that some disaster had come upon her child. Yet though she flew swift as a hawk to the place, she found only the weeping nymphs who could tell her nothing, and, floating on the water where Cyane had stood, Persephone's girdle.

Then Demeter flung a black veil over her head, hiding the brightness of her hair, and so dressed in mourning, set out to search for her child. For nine days she wandered through many

lands; for nine nights she searched by the light of torches which she lit at the volcano's fire. Everywhere she asked the same question. "Have you seen my daughter, Persephone of the slender ankles, a girl with golden hair?" Old Hecate, the witch goddess, had heard a child cry, but no one else could give her an answer.

Then Demeter remembered the Sun, who drives his fiery horses across the sky from morning to night and from whose burning eye nothing is hidden. "Sun," she called, staring full up into the noonday blaze, "answer me truly or my heart will break. Where is Persephone?" When the Sun saw the mother's tears and her weary tread, he was filled with pity for her sorrow and told her the truth at last. "Zeus has given your child to his dark brother Hades to be his wife," he said, "to be queen of ghosts and sit beside him on his black throne in the kingdom of the dead." Demeter stood still as a stone in the rich plain of Sicily. Then in the grief and anger of her heart she tore her hair, making a vow. "Tell the gods that since they have allowed this wicked thing to be, I will not live among them. Nor will I bless the olive, nor smile upon the vine, nor let the corn sprout in the earth until I see my child again."

The months passed and the children of men laboured, but Demeter was seen no more. She would not walk beside the patient oxen when the ploughman drove his long straight furrow across the land. The harvesters looked in vain for her shadow, for her golden grain upon the barren sunlit fields, hard as bronze under their tread. Women and girls wept ritual tears in their weeping cups to call down rain, but still the sky glared white and empty. When autumn came and the woman were still lamenting, she locked up the earth with the iron key of frost. Men and beasts sickened and died, for the goddess who had fed them with a mother's hand now turned her face away from them.

Zeus sent his messenger, the rainbow Iris, who swiftly leapt the gulf between sky and earth. "Zeus asks you to return to Mount Olympus," said the rainbow, in the silken murmur of one brief shower, which raised the hopes of all the thirsty land. Demeter would not yield. Then all the gods came down in turn

The Stealing of Persephone

bringing her splendid gifts, but still she cursed the earth, sitting alone and wasting away with grief for her child. At last Zeus spoke himself. "You may have Persephone again," he said, "but on one condition, that she has not tasted the forbidden food of the dead."

Then, at the command of Zeus, Hermes the messenger plunged like an eagle from high Olympus to the underworld beneath the earth. He went boldly on through dark caverns and tunnels of mist, until he came to a high hall where torchlight flickered on walls polished black as coal. Before him on a throne sat Hades, King of the Dead, and beside him a woman veiled and still. Hecate of the howling dogs attended her, even the pale ghosts feared her, yet this dread queen was still the young girl Persephone. "Hades," said the messenger, "Zeus commands that you send back Persephone to her mother, or Demeter will let the whole earth starve.":   Hades, though a king, dared not disobey the command of his brother, Zeus the Thunderer. Dark and scowling as he was, he smiled a secret smile and stealthily took a pomegranate fruit. "Go, Persephone," he said. "Remember me with kindness when you are in the light of the sun, and to show there is no ill-will in your heart against me, share this pomegranate." He put a slice of fruit swiftly into her mouth, and as though in a dream she swallowed it. For this reason peasant women in Sicily still give pomegranates to their lovers, to compel them to return.

Hermes led Persephone through underground caves, over land, over sea, across underground mountains and deep silent valleys, while the wind roared past them, and with every step Persephone returned to life again. Demeter saw them far off and rushed through the olive trees to meet them, her hair streaming behind her like the mane of some wild creature. Persephone, when she saw her mother, ran to meet her and flung her arms around her neck. Yet even in this joy cold fear touched the mother's heart, and she begged, "Tell me, oh tell me that you did not eat the forbidden food of the dead while you were in the underworld! For if you did, you are in death's power."

Then Persephone remembered the slice of pomegranate,

and wept aloud at the cunning of Hades. "He forced me to eat against my will," she cried. But Zeus decreed that though Persephone must spend a third of the year in the darkness of the earth with her husband, she should return each spring to her mother. And when Hades promised he would come each year to bring her home, she dried her eyes and was comforted.

So each year Persephone, like the seed corn, is hidden in the darkness under the earth. At her going the leaves wither and fall from the trees, the plants shrivel, and the earth grows cold. But when Persephone rises in the golden corn from the earth, Demeter covers the world with green to welcome her. When the year is fulfilled and wheat lies in heaps on the threshing floor, Demeter stands smiling by the threshers, with sheaves of corn and poppies in her hands. So all men honour the Mother and the Daughter, who give them life and food.

Orpheus in the Underworld

ONLY one man was ever bold enough to go down of his own free will to the dark land of the dead. Most men feared to speak the name of Hades; instead they called him the Rich One, because gold and silver were buried in his earth, or the Lord of many Guests, because all men come to his house in the end. But Orpheus went while he was still living to the underworld and returned to tell what he had seen.

Orpheus was a musician. He served the garlanded Apollo, who grants men healing from pain and sickness, who teaches his worshippers immortal music and writes the law of kindness in their hearts. This god gave Orpheus a lyre with seven gold strings and taught him to play it as no man ever has or ever will play. When Orpheus set his hand to the lyre, all men stopped to listen. The patient beasts of burden, the donkey in the fields, the ox at the plough stood still. The wild beasts were spellbound by the music. The wolf forgot to howl to the echoing hills, the deer and the swift hare stood still, the snake stretched his length in the grass and the lizard on the rock; even snail the house-carrier stopped his slow crawl to listen. Trees dragged up their roots to follow Orpheus as he went playing over the hills, and the mountains bent their freezing heads to listen.

Orpheus married a lovely nymph, Eurydice, and the god of marriages himself came to their feast. Yet he did not sing his usual song to greet the bride, and the torch he carried sputtered and smoked, bringing tears to the eyes. All feared this foretold sorrow, and so it happened. The new bride went walking in the cool and shadowy vale of Tempe under Mount Olympus. There she trod on a snake, hidden in the long grass, which poured its angry venom into her young veins. So, untimely, Eurydice died. Her soul could not live without the body which was its home, but fled to the underworld, where the shades of the dead drift in pale companies, like fallen leaves. It is black grief to know that thus our lives must end. Orpheus would not submit to it. Boldly he vowed to go down to the land of the dead and bring his young wife back again.

He slung his lyre on his back, and set out at once, through a dark cavern in the mountains of Thrace, which all men know is a gateway to Hades. Down the dank shaft he climbed into the caverns of the underworld; the sound of birds came from further and further away, the scent of grass faded and darkness thickened around him. In the depths of the rock it grew cold; he heard an underground stream, then came to a black, slow-circling river, the Styx, which flows nine times around the shore of Hades. On it floated a rotting boat, rowed by a grizzled and surly old boatman. This was Charon, who would leave a soul forever wandering on the river-bank if the friends of the dead man were too poor to put a coin in his mouth for the fare, yet when Orpheus played his lute, Charon silently made room in the boat and rowed him across the dark water. On the far bank waited a huge brindled mastiff, with three snarling, foam-flecked heads ready to bite, the watchdog Cerberus. Yet when Orpheus played, the brute slunk out and licked his feet with three rough tongues. Orpheus strode boldly on into the kingdom of the dead.

Before him sat three judges on three thrones. They sternly question every dying soul and order rest or punishment as it deserves. Sins in the world above are judged in the world below and meet sure doom. Around the judges stood the ghosts awaiting judgement. There, thin shadow of her living self, still pale and limping from her wound, stood Eurydice. There was neither light nor darkness in that place but a dull, even grey, no scent of living plant, no trees but Persephone's grove of black poplars. The river of forgetfulness flowed there. Whoever drank from it forgot all that was past in the world above. Joys and sorrows both vanished in mist. Day and night, times and seasons, love and hate had no meaning in the sadness of that place. Yet Orpheus took his lyre and plucked the strings, as simply as when he played to his friends after supper on summer nights. The ghosts drifted round him to listen.

Eurydice had not yet drunk from the river of forgetfulness; she knew her husband's music at once and came to his side. The three dread judges sat silent, heads bowed to listen: even those they had condemned were freed for a while from their torments. Forty-nine sisters who had murdered their husbands no longer carried endless jars of water to fill a giant sieve. The king who killed his own son no longer stood hungry and thirsty among fruit trees, by a lake which vanished at his touch. The crafty thief no longer sweated and panted to roll a vast boulder up an endless hill. For a time all these knew rest, while Orpheus played.

Then there was a stirring, like dry leaves in the wind, among the thin ghosts. King Hades and his queen, Persephone, had come out of their palace to listen. Now Orpheus played and sang for them. His music began softly, then rang loudly through the grey air. Hades leaned forward on his throne; Persephone sat still, head bent to listen. "We men and women," he sang, "with all we have, belong to you. In death we come to you; yours is our longest home. Eurydice would have come to you at last, but you took her from me too soon, before her time. Either give her back or take me also, for I will not live without her." Hades was grim and mournful, but severely just, a dread but not an evil god; besides, he too had known the pain of love. Some even say Persephone pleaded with him for these young lovers. At last Hades spoke. "Take Eurydice," he said, "and go, on one condition. Do not look back at her until she is safely under the light of the sun."

Orpheus turned and went towards the great gate, while Eurydice followed slowly, still faint and limping from her poisoned wound. Out of the high double gates they went; past the dog Cerberus, which lay quietly, its three heads on its paws, over the black river with the silent boatman. Through the dark underground tunnels they went, and into the cave, impatient now for the sunlight and the living breath of air. Almost on the threshold Orpheus felt the stab of sudden fear. Had Eurydice followed him safely, or had she fallen, lame and faint as she was, far back in the maze of underground caverns? He listened, but could not hear her ghostly footfall on the stones. He turned to look. She was there, close behind him. He stretched out eager arms to hold her, but she began to fade before his eyes. He called to her, but she wavered and dissolved, like smoke down the wind. His hands held emptiness; Eurydice had returned to night.

Now there was no hope left for Orpheus. He rushed after the shade of his wife to the brink of the Styx, but now the surly boatman pushed him aside, without a word or a glance, while the ghost of Eurydice already sat shuddering in the leaky boat. On the far bank Cerberus snarled a triple warning. For seven days Orpheus sat mourning on that dark shore, without sleeping or tasting food. Then slowly he returned to the world. The very stones pitied him.

Yet Orpheus had learnt wisdom from his journey to the underworld, for now he sang different songs, while the trees gathered in a circle to give him shade and the beasts lay around his feet to listen. He sang that earth and sky were one; they parted and warred but re-wedded and together brought to life all things. The gods above the snows are their children; so are trees and green plants, birds, beasts of all kinds, fish that breathe the seas, and all the tribes of men. Gods, beasts, and men are all nature's children, all bound by her laws. The same sky shines over all, and all should live like brothers. No Greek had ever shaped such thoughts before, and many good men tried to live by the teaching of Orpheus.

Orpheus met a dreadful death. Every year at the time of the grape harvest, the women worshippers of the wine god,

Dionysus, drank and danced themselves into frenzy. A band of these maddened creatures caught sight of Orpheus and attacked him, tearing him apart with savage teeth and nails, till the stones ran red with his blood. The beasts had heard and understood him, yet these degraded women let his last breath slip away, unheard as the wind. The grieving birds, the wild creatures, and the woods that had so often heard his music, all wept for Orpheus. The trees shed their leaves and went bareheaded, the rivers flooded with autumn weight of tears. The bright-haired nymphs of tree and fountain mourned, and nightingales sang a dirge where he had walked.

Apollo put his lyre as a constellation among the stars; but the ghost of Orpheus went down content to the underworld. The three judges of the dead decreed that through all his life he had been wise and generous, fit to enter Elysium, the fields of the blessed. There storm, snow or rain never come, but a soft wind to cool the brows of heroes, and calm happiness at the world's end. There Orpheus searched till he had found Eurydice and clasped her at last in eager arms.

Heroes and Monsters

Perseus in the Chest

ACRISIUS was reigning king of Argos. He had fought his brother for the kingdom and built himself a citadel, high on a rock looking out to sea at Tiryns. Yet Acrisius lacked one thing; he had no son to follow him, only one young daughter, Danae. He went to seek counsel at the shrine of an oracle, but the hollow voice of the god spoke through the priestess's gold mask in words of ill omen. "You will never have a son, and the grandson you will have must kill you." All the dusty road home, Acrisius brooded in fear and cunning.

At last he decided in self defence that Danae must never love a man and never bear a child. He built a strong tower of brass, chained savage dogs at the door, took the lovely girl out of the sunshine and locked her inside. Danae could see from her high window other people going about the city: to the running track, to the theatre, to market, or leading the garlanded beast in procession to the temple. She could hear distant shouts and the noise of flutes playing for weddings and dances, but no happy song would ever be sung at her wedding. Unseen and unheard by all men, she wept. But Zeus, who sees all things from his thunder chariot, saw Danae in her desolate tower.

One night, of all the endless nights, Danae took from her

body its gold chains, bracelets and rings, loosened her long hair and let slip the pleated robe from her shoulders. As she lay down to sleep, she saw in the moonlight shimmering flakes of gold fall on her body, with touch as soft as snow. So rain had fallen on the earth at the beginning of the world, bringing fertility and new life. At midnight, not knowing what she did, Danae welcomed the greatest of the gods in a shower of gold as her lover.

Earth after rain had given birth to men, and Danae, as the seasons went round, gave birth to a son. She named him Perseus, first of the heroes, and found him a lovely sorrow. She who had known the pleasures of love with a god, now knew its pains. For Acrisius, when he learnt that Danae had borne the grandson who must kill him, was consumed in the torment of his fear. He dared not kill Danae and her baby, for the Furies hunt down those who harm their own flesh and blood to the uttermost ends of time and space; there is no escaping their vengeance. Yet he must rid himself of the child, so endearingly small, so huge a threat to his life.

He found in the cellars of the citadel a massive bronze-bound chest. His men at arms, fearful for their own lives, crammed Danae and the child into the box and slammed the lid with a heavy crash. The girl neither pleaded nor wept, recognizing fate. Silently she curved her body, to shield her son, as they dragged the chest to the harbour's edge and heaved it into the sea.

At first the wooden chest skimmed the waves like a bird, riding the crests and plunging into steep troughs. Then a storm seized them, with driving spray and roaring winter skies. Yet still the child slept, and Danae spoke to him as he lay in her arms. "My dearest babe, what cruel sorrow is yours, and yet you do not cry. You are not afraid of the salt foam or the shrieking winds; you sleep in this dark chest on the waters as though you were rocking in your polished cradle in a king's palace. Truly the gods must protect you, or you have a godlike heart." All night long the chest rocked in the dark, as by the will of Zeus it cut a pathway through the sea. The wind dropped and the sea-mist lifted; morning came, a beautiful

Perseus in the Chest

still day. A scent of trees and wild herbs wafted far out over the water. Danae, alert for her child's life, could smell land, though she could not yet see it. They had travelled sixty miles to Seriphus.

Seriphus was one of those small islands scattered in handfuls through the dark blue Aegean Sea. Poseidon sends his breakers to thunder and surge against the cliffs; the people cling for their lives to its high headlands and scratch a living from the bare rock. That morning a fisherman named Dictys was early at the rock-bound harbour. He was brother to the chief of the island, for in the days of the heroes every man toiled with his own hands. Dictys had been out all night, fishing by torchlight, and now was sitting on a rock, mending his nets with swift brown fingers. He saw a chest drifting off-shore, and dragged it in, hoping for treasure from some wreck of the night's storm. But when he prised open the lock and forced the creaking hinges, he found a young woman, with a beautiful child, awake now and watching him with darkly shining eyes. "We were cast adrift in freezing misfortune," said the mother, "but destiny has set us in bright day again, if you will be our friend."

Dictys, a good and simple man, took them to his home. A hut of whitewashed clay stood under a poplar's shade; nets hung by the door and a stream of clear water trickled down to the strand. Here Perseus grew to manhood, eating the rough, healthy food of the poor: bean soup and barley bread rubbed with a raw onion, goat's cheese, figs and honey. He worked with Dictys at man's work, rowing the fishing boat, drawing in the heavy nets with their leaping silver harvest, digging for water at midsummer in the iron-hard earth. He grew superb in body, bold in heart. At cliff-climbing, swimming and hunting he led the young men of the island.

When the people met for festival games, racing, wrestling, boxing or throwing the heavy bronze disc, Perseus won the laurel crown. The watchers threw garlands round his feet, honouring the gifts of beauty and courage, which only the gods can give. The chief of the island watched Perseus and before long caught sight of his mother. Danae was now in the summer of her beauty, that proud season when face and body bear the mind's impress. At once the petty tyrant of the island desired her for his own. He took her, a king's daughter, for a slave in his rough household, and tried to force marriage on her but she proudly refused. For men dare all things if they have freedom in their hearts and are not slaves to possessions. Perseus stood by to defend his mother with his life, a man to be feared, for all his poverty. "From his manners one might think him a king's son!" muttered the chief resentfully in his beard.

The island chieftain plotted to rid himself of Zeus's proud son. He pretended that he meant to marry another woman, and asked the free men of Seriphus to contribute one horse each to the bride-price. "Ours is a small barren island," he said, "but I will not shame it by cutting a poor figure among the rich princes of the mainland." He wove a cunning web of words before them all and ended, "Surely you will help me, noble Perseus?" This was a well-wrought insult, for he knew Perseus had nothing but his two strong hands. But the sons of gods cannot be shamed, and Perseus laughed in his face. "I have neither horse nor gold," he said cheerfully. "But if you really intend to marry another wife and leave my mother in peace, then I wish you such joy, I will give you any gift you care to name." And his destiny, calling from the future, made him add, laughing, "Even Medusa's head if you want it!"

The chief heard him with fearful joy; he could hardly believe his good fortune. For Medusa the Terrifying One wore the mask of fear personified; the cold glitter of her eyes turned men to stone. "I should like that better than any wedding present in the world," said the tyrant swiftly, while all his followers broke into shouts of mocking laughter. Perseus strode proudly out of the hall, head high, step firm, though inwardly cursing his own rash words. Not one man there expected to see him again. They did not know the breed of the gods.

Perseus slays the Gorgon

PERSEUS had to fulfil his promise to cut off the head of Medusa, the Gorgon, or know that all men laughed at him as a boaster and a coward. He stood on the cliffs and looked across the sea. Beyond the horizon lived the Gorgons, three terrible winged sisters with the bodies of women, serpent-hair and cruel claws of brass. No one returned to tell of them, for all who saw them froze in stony dread, the petrification of terror. "Athena, help me!" cried Perseus inwardly. "Give me your strength and cunning to do what I have promised, or I shall be put to shame before all men." A light shone in the sky, so brilliant that Perseus covered his face against its blinding rays. Then, fearfully, he raised his head.

The light shone from a great gold shield, polished bright as a looking-glass to reflect the sun. The woman who held it was taller than any mortal man and looked down on Perseus from her great height with shining grey eyes. Beside her stood a young man carrying a sickle of glittering black obsidian, harder than iron, the first deadly weapon of the ancient world. His feet seemed hardly to touch the earth, for at the heel of each golden boot quivered a pair of living wings. By these signs Perseus recognized Athena, bringer of counsel, and

Hermes, messenger of the gods. He did not know these immortals were his sister and brother, since all three were born of Zeus. In awe and dread he fell upon his knees before them.

"Look into the shield," said a voice. Perseus looked. Slowly a face appeared in the polished circle, a woman's features, but ageless, livid, surrounded by knots of writhing snakes. Two evil basilisks looked out from the hair on her temples, and her own eyes glittered with a cold, reptilian light. "That is the Gorgon, the Terrible One," said Athena's clear, grave voice. "Do you still dare to face her and her sisters?"

Perseus shuddered, but godlike pride mingled with his mortal blood. Remembering his boast, he answered stoutly "I do." "Then take this shield," said the goddess. "Do not turn your eyes towards Medusa, but watch her image in the shield's reflection, and so strike safely." Then she gave him a leather satchel to hang from his shoulder. "Cut off her head and put it in this bag." Hermes put the shining sickle into his right hand, and unbound the winged boots from his own feet. "These boots of mine will carry you over land and sea" he said with a shrewd and friendly glance; "and this sword will slay the Gorgon with a single stroke. Only remember; never look at her." Then he gave Perseus a black helmet, with frowning visor. "This is the helmet of darkness, lent to you by Hades," he said. "Put it on and you will be invisible." "How shall I find Medusa?" asked Perseus, for in all his life he had never left the little island. Athena pointed with her long bronze spear. "Go northwards," she said, "beyond the home of the north wind, to the three grey sisters who have only one eye and one tooth between them. They will tell you the way."

The two immortals vanished into the wide air, leaving Perseus to bind on the boots and begin his journey alone. Northward he went winging through the vast skies, by sunlight and starlight, for seven days and nights. He did not know his sister goddess flew by his side, hidden among the clouds. He saw what no man living had seen before. He looked down from the heights of heaven to the many-coloured earth. Lands and seas wheeled back beneath his winged feet, until he found himself at last on the shores of darkness. In that land of endless

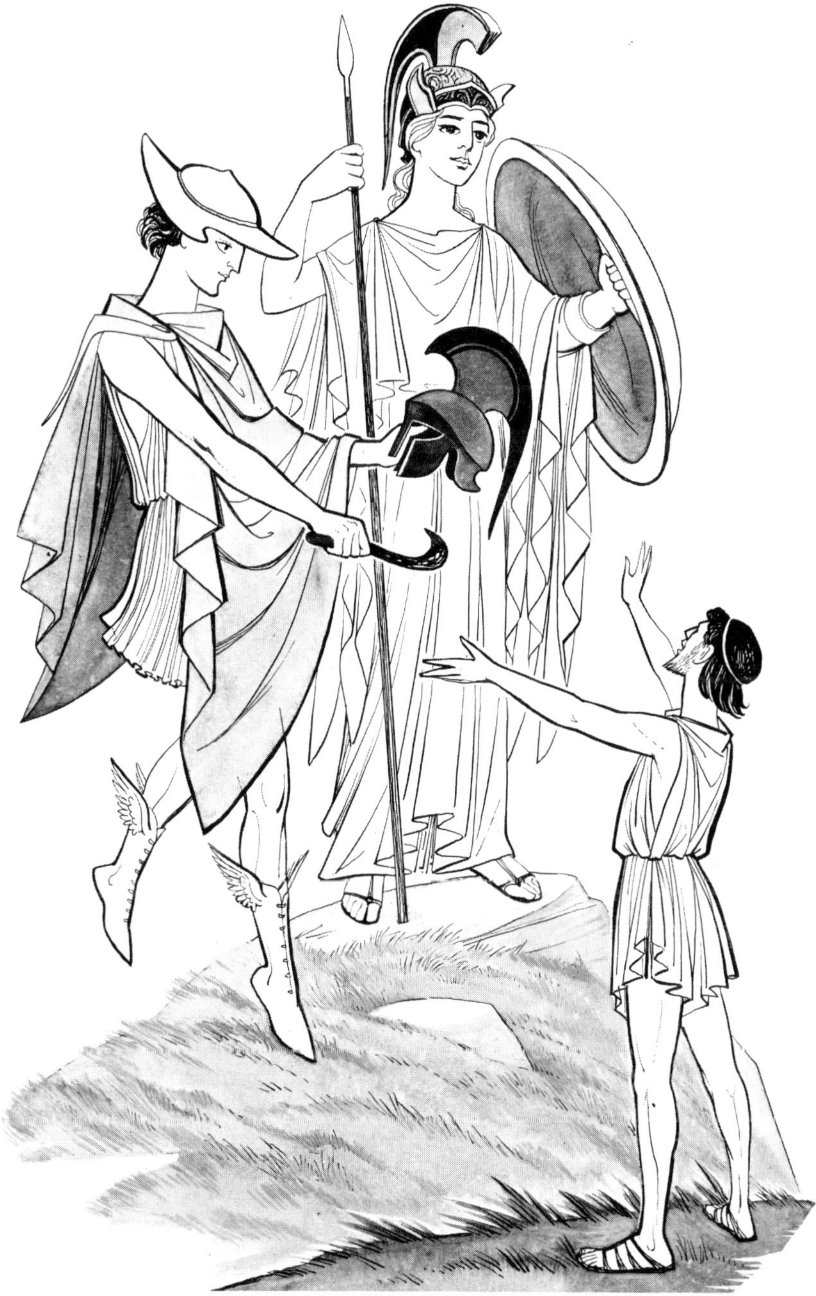

polar night, great snowflakes drifted slowly down under the freezing moon. The air was filled with the song of three grey hags who sat by the frozen sea. They passed their one tooth from hand to hand and groped blindly after the single eye. They sensed a shivering in the air and set up a thin screeching, but not even the eye could see Perseus, for he wore Hades's helmet of invisibility.

"Save me, O helmet of Hades," prayed Perseus. He feared the three sisters, for he knew they were kin to the three Fates who control the thread of each man's destiny. Nevertheless, he crept stealthily towards them, and put out his strong, brown, young hand. The hags clutched blindly at him, but he leapt back out of their reach and shouted,"I have your eye, o cruel blind sisters! Tell me the way to the Gorgons' land, or I will throw your moonlight into the sea of darkness for ever!" The three sisters cursed, beat their meagre breasts and lamented, but they were forced at last to answer the question.

"Fly westward to the garden of the sunset," they cried. "There you will find the singing nymphs of the golden apple tree. They will tell you the way to the Gorgon. The end of it will be that for all your daring she will turn you to stone!" Perseus flung the single eye back to them and leapt into the sky, treading the air with his winged boots as he soared upwards, glad to leave that place of darkness behind.

He flew westward into the setting sun, while clouds flamed round his feet and the grey waves of the sea shone gold beneath him. He landed at last on a lonely island, echoing with song, where he wandered through twilit orchards, under one high, bright star. This was the garden of the sunset. Far off he heard the singing, too sweet and strange for mortal voices, and knew these were the nymphs he had come to seek, sunset's daughters, whose evening magic turns common day to gold. He stepped out from the grove and saw them circling hand in hand, to the music of their own singing, round a tree hung with golden apples. Coiled round the trunk, an ancient dragon watched them with unblinking eyes.

Perseus stepped courteously towards them. "O lovely-haired daughters of sunset," he said, "pray tell me where to

Perseus slays the Gorgon

find Medusa." "Medusa, the Terrible One!" cried the nymphs, wringing their slender hands. "She will turn you to stone!" They clung to the handsome young mortal, twined soft arms around him and tried to hold him back, but Perseus gently freed himself. When they saw his mind was made up, the nymphs pointed sorrowfully to the south. "There beyond the end of Ocean is the island where the Gorgons live. Many brave men have set out to conquer them, but none has ever returned. Farewell for ever, dear young hero!"

Perseus, took Hermes's shining sickle and Athena's shield, hung the leather satchel from his strong shoulders, and leapt into the air. Below him the song of the nymphs faded under the rushing wind. The winged boots carried him far out into the ocean of the setting sun, where sky and sea swim in each other's arms. At last, on the horizon, he saw a scattered handful of islands. Around them the waves broke in a tangle of foam over rocks the size and shape of men; these were the brave travellers who had never returned. Below him Perseus heard the rustle of scaly wings and knew that he had found the home of the Terrible Ones. It was time for him to turn his eyes away, or become another rock, petrified in an agony of dread. "Save me, o shield of Athena," prayed Perseus, as treading the blue air with winged heels he looked steadfastly into the polished shield.

The reptile-bird-women lay sleeping in their lair below him. Medusa tossed in her sleep and the rank smell of carrion rose from her plumage. The claws of brass at each wing tip glittered in the sunlight as they lay folded across her breast. With a brief prayer to the gods, Perseus, still watching in the shield, swooped on long wings of courage towards the sleeping Gorgons. The snakes in Medusa's hair woke, reared their heads and began to hiss at the sound of his flight.

She opened scaly eyelids and turned her cold glance upon him, but Perseus would not meet her eyes. Steadily, with all the strength of his will, he looked into the shield. Then, having judged the danger, he said to himself, "Success without risk is not honoured." He thought of the seas and lands he had looked down on from on high and the stars towards which he had soared on beating wings; he knew at last that every man who meets danger unafraid becomes in part a god. He gained height, swooped again and with fast, crafty twists and turns beat down Medusa's flailing wings. As she lay panting for breath, he raised the sword of Hermes, judged the distance in his shield, and swiftly brought it down upon her neck, severing the snaky head with one clean cut. Fearless still, he caught up the head by its feebly writhing knots, dropped it into his leather bag, and sprang into the air.

But the panting and hissing of the fight had awakened the Gorgon's two sisters. They smelt snake's blood, saw the headless body of Medusa lying with crumpled wings upon the rocks and knew that murder had been done. They leapt up with a terrible cry, baring their claws, spread scaly bat-wings and made after Perseus as he flew. "Save me now, O boots of Hermes," prayed Perseus, soaring up into the clouds, while the rattle of the Gorgons' wings pursued him. He sped over the sea, where dolphins circled far below, blowing water-spouts from their nostrils. His beautiful bright hair streamed out behind him as he flew, faster than thought.

The Gorgons raced after him across the sky, hissing and grinding their teeth with rage, as the clang of his bronze sword against the shield grew faint in the distance. The howls of the age-old monsters faded from his ears, and Perseus knew that he had escaped their vengeance. Then he hoisted the leather strap of the satchel on his shoulder, turned his face to the east and beat his way on whirring wings across Africa. Drops of black blood dripped from the leather bag to the earth, from which grew the many snakes of that dark continent. But Perseus flew, glorious and unafraid. The gods looked down from the shining porch of Olympus and smiled on their young kinsman, whose deeds were worthy of his birth.

Perseus and the Sea Monster

PERSEUS flew onward. The sea coast of north Africa faded behind him to a shining line. The orange groves of the fertile coast gave way to olive trees, then to dry river-beds and long tawny ridges of sand. Before him Perseus saw the giant shape of Atlas, the Titan who holds up the sky. Atlas was weary, his shoulders bowed under the weight of suns and stars. As Perseus sank lightly to earth, the Titan reached out huge hands to seize him. "Stranger," he shouted in a voice that shook the sky, "are you the hero who will one day come to set me free?" Perseus shook his bright head. "Then what," boomed the Titan, "do you keep in that bag?" For answer, Perseus turned his own head away and loosened the leather thongs, showing Medusa's face. At the sight the Titan slowly petrified with horror into a mountain, his head the rocky peak, his giant arms the ridges, his legs the foothills, half buried in sand. Where he stood in the desert, the Atlas Mountains thrust into the sky, their summits lost in snow and cloud. So the old Titan rested at last from his labours, as you may see to this day.

Perseus, who had watched all this, took up his bag and sword again, bound on the winged boots and cut his way through the burning air. From west to east he flew, across the whole breadth of Africa, over countless tribes and peoples, whose lands spread out beneath his feet. He flew over Egypt, where the great pyramids already stood by the Nile, and rounded the coast of Asia Minor. The hungry sea beat on the cliffs like a devouring monster, eating the life-giving land away.

Then, tiny in the distance, Perseus saw what looked like a human figure, chained to the cliffs in the sea's path. Down plunged the young hero, the wind whistling in his ears with the speed of his flight. Seen near at hand, the figure was a young African girl, naked, but hung with rich barbaric jewels. She was perfect and Perseus thought at first she must be a black marble statue, but the light wind stirred her cloudy hair and real tears streamed from her eyes. Awed by her naked beauty, Perseus stood still in wonder, almost forgetting to hover in the air with his wings. "Tell me your name, o glorious young goddess," he said, "and the name of your country, and why you are in chains."

Then the lovely African girl spoke through her tears. She was Princess Andromeda, daughter of the king of Ethiopia, whose lands stretched from the sources of the Nile to the Middle Sea. Her mother, a beautiful but vain and foolish woman, had boasted that she was more beautiful than the sea-nymphs. Poseidon was angry at this challenge to his daughters. In revenge he ate away the cliffs and sent salt water swirling over the fertile land, to leave a barren desert. The Ethiopians poured offerings of oil on the troubled waters, and begged the sea with sobs and tears to relent before they starved. Poseidon promised at last that he would cease to eat away the coast, if Andromeda were chained to the cliffs for one of his sea monsters to devour.

Even before the princess had finished her strange story, there was a roaring in the sea like a tidal wave, and a huge shape rose from the waters. The girl screamed. Unseen, Athena breathed strength and daring into the body of Perseus, making him strong-handed, lithe-limbed, with valour in his eyes and victory as his destiny. "Do not weep, lovely Andromeda," he shouted. "I killed the scaly Gorgon, and will save your life!"

Perseus and the Sea Monster

He sprang from the earth, and shot high into the clouds, watching the tidal monster as it surged towards land. Huge as a ship, it reared above the salt waves, thrashing the water with mottled coils; rearing a scaly head, it looked this way and that, pale jaws streaming foam ready to engulf everything in its path. Suddenly it saw the moving shadow of Perseus upon the shining waters, veered and made after it angrily, with snapping white teeth. Like Zeus's own eagle, Perseus swooped from the sky, holding steady the sickle of Hermes which had cut off Medusa's head. Through narrowed eyes he judged his mark, and aiming for the monster's streaming neck, buried the sickle up to its hilt. The tidal monster, maddened by its wound, reared in the air, high as a ship's mast, then fell with a thunderous crash, churning the foam in wide circles. Perseus danced on the air with swift wings, nimble as a prize-fighter, dodging from side to side to escape the frothing jaws, and stabbing wherever he could get beneath the guard to land a blow.

Spray boiled around the two enemies as they fought, hiding them from the watchers on the shore. Perseus's plumage grew drenched and heavy; he could not trust the wings at his heels to bear him up any longer and almost feared the sea would overwhelm him. Then he remembered the cliff climbs on Seriphus when he was a boy and wedged himself firmly against a jutting rock.

The monster was tiring now, its heaves and struggles growing weaker as its life blood stained the green sea red. Perseus watched it narrowly, waiting his time. Three times, four times, he drove his weapon home in its neck. Black waves of death spouted from its mouth; the fish-tail thrashed for the last time, the shiny coils fell slack on the water, and the crowd on the cliffs raised a great shout of joy as the monster sank dead under the waves of the now quiet sea. Even the gods looking down from Olympus shouted to see their young hero, with glory crowning his bright hair.

Pride, the breaker of men, was not in Perseus. He cut Andromeda loose from her chains, knowing when to use gentleness and be used by it. Then he stripped, and washed himself clean of sweat and blood in a rock pool. Next he built altars on the shore, to offer thanks to his helpers, Hermes and Athena, and to his unknown father, Zeus. Andromeda, when she saw the young man's glorious body and the godlike fearlessness which was born in him, when she felt the tender touch of his hands which had slain monsters, knew the force of love. Perseus stood in wonder before the rich prize her hands and lips offered. Aphrodite rising from the sea had taken swift possession of them both.

The Ethiopians held a great marriage feast for Perseus and Andromeda. They flung wide the palace doors, hung wedding garlands from the roof, threw incense on the flames and sang the bride's song with a happy heart. Even the daughters of Ocean were contented, for where Perseus had laid down the Gorgon's head, seaweed had turned to coral, making wreathed jewels for their hair. Now Perseus, who had travelled so far, longed to see his home again. He took Andromeda in his arms and flew back through light and darkness to the wave-beaten island of Seriphus. They landed on the cliffs, unbound the winged boots and walked hand in hand to the town. Danae was not to be seen, nor was Dictys mending his nets on the shore; both had fled to the temple to take sanctuary from the king's anger. Perseus strode to the citadel, where the chieftain was drinking with his followers.

"Welcome, my dear boy," said the false smiler. "And have you brought the wedding present you promised me?" For answer Perseus opened the satchel, eyes closed, to show his gruesome gift. The Gorgon stared at the company with stony eyes. As the king met their gaze, a shudder ran through him, and his living flesh turned to cold stone. The terrible head struck his followers stone dead with him, and their weather-worn circle stands on the island to this day. So Perseus avenged Danae's long slavery and forced love, bringing to Seriphus the doom the gods had written. Dictys became ruler in his brother's place, and Danae, seeing her glorious son, knew for a certainty that his father had been a god.

Then Perseus showed true wisdom. He had felt the gods all around him on his journeys. In hard trials he had felt their

Perseus and the Sea Monster

power within himself. He had lived like a god, yet now he was content to become mortal again. He gave Medusa's head to Athena, who fixed it on her golden shield to petrify her enemies. He gave back the sickle of obsidian, the helmet of darkness and the winged shoes. Now he would walk the dusty roads of earth, a man among men. Yet he still had his fate to fulfil. He went to a festival of games on the mainland, where Danae's father Acrisius sat among the watchers on the stone benches. Perseus threw the disc in contest with the young men; but a sudden buffet of wind and the force of fate drove his disc among the crowd, killing his grandfather on the spot. So all the cruel scheming of Acrisius went for nothing; no man can hide from destiny.

Perseus was greatly grieved, for royal Danae had never spoken ill to him of her father. He buried Acrisius with kingly honours, beside the temple of Athena. Now Perseus ruled in his grandfather's place as king of Argos, and built a great fortress on the hilltop at Mycenae. Its ramparts were made of **stones so huge that men said the Cyclopes had been stonemasons.** In its tawny walls are corridors where two men can still walk abreast; bolts big as a man's arm still groove the door-frames. From his terrace Perseus could look out over his kingdom, the orchards, the bare hills, the sea, dark as wine. In his pillared hall the smoke rose day and night from a friendly hearth and his gates stood open to travellers. The tales of all he did were long and his honours were as many as the stones of the sea.

Time treated Perseus with kindness. He knew enduring strength and happy old age. Base lies and shrill jealousy were never heard in his house, for Perseus and Andromeda were loving and faithful all their lives. They had many children, among them, it is said, the rulers of Persia. No stormy wind of autumn overwhelmed them, no stone of envy struck them; when they died they left their children a name of which no ill was ever spoken. "Truly," wrote the teller of this tale, "happiness stays with men, when a god has helped its planting."

Heracles the Young Hero

WHEN Heracles was ten months old his mother the lady Alcmena put him to bed one night with Iphicles, his twin brother. Iphicles was the son of a warrior lord, Amphitryon of Argos, but Heracles outshone his brother in strength and beauty, for he was the son of Zeus. Blue-eyed Alcmena was the tallest and fairest of women, true and generous of heart. Zeus had chosen her among all women to bear a son strong and brave enough to free mankind from all monsters and dangers.

Alcmena bathed the two boys in a steaming wooden tub, dried them with soft woollen cloths upon her knees and suckled them herself like a peasant woman. She wrapped them in clean bands and laid them side by side in a huge bronze shield, which she rocked from side to side with her foot, like a cradle, until the even breathing of the two children told her they were both asleep. In those heroic days of the warriors with bronze swords, even the lords of Greece lived as simply as shepherds; Alcmena as mistress of a large household had many duties.

She tended her children with her own hands like any woman of the people. She spun the fleece of Amphitryon's ewes on her own silver distaff and sent her fifty women slaves searching the countryside for blue iris and red madder roots to dye the homespun yarn. Walking behind her loom, she wove the cloth for fine tunics, the fleecy rugs to cover the beds and the broad tapestries that hung upon the walls in winter. She went with her women when they carried the household washing to the stream, trod the linen in the water with them and helped them spread it on the stones to bleach in the sun. She watched the house slaves to see the high hall was swept each day, the bronze lamps refilled with oil, the corn meal ground between heavy stones and the water jars filled at the well.

Now as soon as she saw that her children were sleeping, she went softly from the room to the hall. There Amphitryon's soldiers and huntsmen sat drinking on benches round the walls, while the roasting meat smoked and hissed on the central hearth. She carved the boar's flesh with her own hands, set it before her husband and mixed his wine with honey to sweeten it. Then the women set up bedsteads under the gallery of the hall for servants and strangers together, darkness came, and everyone in the house lay down to sleep.

At midnight Alcmena woke suddenly. It seemed to her she heard a cry. She listened again; this time it was clear, Iphicles was screaming with fear or pain. As she listened a strange light flared up in the dark house; through the open doorway she could see the piled-up armour glinting and the pillars of polished cypress in the great hall shining red as fire. "Wake up, wake up, Amphitryon!" she cried leaping from bed naked as she lay. "Zeus has sent the light to warn us of some danger!" The unearthly gleam wavered and died away. "Torches," shouted Amphitryon, reaching for his sword on its peg on the wall. The house slaves who slept in the hall and the corridors woke at his call. They kindled sticks from embers of the hearth and came running with these torches in their hands: Barefoot and tousled with sleep, they crowded after Amphitryon as he strode through the hall to the alcove where the children lay. Alcmena, following, shrieked with horror at what she saw. Zeus had indeed sent the light as a warning of danger to his son. For jealous Hera had seen the boy from her golden throne, and angry at heart because Zeus loved his mother, had sent danger to destroy him.

Two serpents had writhed their way into the house and twisted themselves round the body of Heracles as he lay sleeping in his shield cradle. Now they were tightening their scaly coils to crush him to death. Their eyes shone with hateful fire, their heads were poised to strike and their forked tongues darted towards his face. "My son!" cried Alcmena in anguish. The slaves huddled in the doorway fell back wailing. Even Amphitryon stood aghast, and Iphicles screamed louder. But Heracles seized the snakes, one in each hand, with the grip of a wrestler and laughed aloud with pleasure at his own strength. It was his first trial by battle.

The serpents writhed and twisted, but could not escape. Heracles tightened his grip on them. Their coils began to fall slack and venom dripped on the stone floor as their murderous jaws gaped, gasping for air. Amphitryon drew his sword, but as he lifted it to strike, Heracles with a shout of triumph flung the two serpents, limp as two coils of rope, at his feet. Their glittering scales grew dull and lustreless in the torchlight, their flickering tongues stiffened in death. Then Alcmena lifted Iphicles, still screaming with fear, and cradling him in her arms carried him to her own bed. With soft words and caresses she lulled him at last to sleep. But Heracles lay alone in the great bronze shield, like a soldier sleeping on the battlefield, and rested peaceful and still as though nothing had happened, till the cocks crowed at morning.

Next day Alcmena asked the advice of a learned priest and set to work like a careful housewife to drive the evil spirits of the two dead serpents from her home. She made a great heap of dry gorse and windblown thorn, and at midnight burnt both snakes to ashes. Country people in many lands still make such winter bonfires, to burn the old year's ill-luck and fertilize the earth for the new year's crops. At dawn Alcmena trampled the wood ash into the soil and returned to the house to burn a cleansing fire of herbs. She set her maids to sweep the hall, and sprinkle water from a blessed bough through all the house. Last of all she sacrificed a young bull

Heracles the Young Hero

to Zeus, with a prayer that her son might triumph always over all his enemies.

She had good cause to fear that Hera would always be his foe, and in this, as it turned out, she was right. Yet for the present no danger showed, and Heracles lived out his boyhood on the wide sunlit plain of Thebes. He played on the floor of the great hall among the soldiers and heard their tales of battle. As soon as he could stand he learnt to grasp their weapons in his childish but powerful hands. He practised wrestling and boxing. A mighty huntsman taught him to shoot with bow and arrows. He learnt how to drive four fiery chariot horses at once, and how to turn corners without grazing the chariot wheels. His bed was set up among the men-at-arms and his only coverlet was the skin of a mountain lion. He wore a short tunic of rough homespun wool like a fighting man. His dinner was of plain roast meat, his bread a barley loaf in a basket, such as labourers eat in the fields, his supper simple as a soldier's in camp. He liked to sleep under the stars better than lying in bed.

At the games, running, wrestling, putting heavy weights, or at the dancing, when the young men danced together, twirling and stamping their feet in the dust, Heracles was first. His eyes flashed fire; his spear never missed its mark. In those days of danger and hard living, a man needed above all to be strong and brave. Yet Heracles was also kind, generous to friends and enemies alike and slow to quarrel. At eighteen years, when he wanted a club for hunting, he chose a shapely wild olive upon Mount Helicon and dragged it up whole by the roots, for he had grown straight and strong as a young tree himself. So passed the boyhood of the hero Heracles.

The Labours of Heracles-I

ALL the heroes mastered ships on the sea and chariots in battle; all were strong of hand and swift of foot and carried their bronze swords into strange lands. But Heracles alone fought for the good of man, toiling to free the earth from monsters and dangers. Therefore among all the sons of gods, men loved Heracles best. No outward force could compel him, and though his body was often wounded, nothing could break his godlike spirit. Hera, jealous that Zeus had slighted her for a mortal woman, would have liked to kill Heracles, but after many angry quarrels with Zeus reached an agreement. If Alcmena's son could perform twelve impossible labours, he should become immortal like his father. Heracles grew to manhood and became a famous soldier, a leader of just men. Where the dust of battle rose, there he was happy and at home. Yet all this time Hera searched for ways to turn his strength against himself.

Heracles married a king's daughter who bore him tall sons and all men called him happy. Then without warning Hera sent raging madness upon him. In the darkness and turmoil of his mind, he saw enemies everywhere, threatening him with naked swords. First he tried to kill his brother's son Iolus, who escaped his wild blows and ran for his life. Then Heracles turned on his own young sons, hunted them down with loud war cries, battered them both to death and threw their bodies into the fire. When he awoke, like a man from nightmare sleep, Heracles found the blood of his own children on his hands. Black grief and shame swept over him. For days on end he locked himself into a dark room, neither eating, sleeping, nor speaking to his friends, but cursing the fatal strength the gods had given him. Then he made a pilgrimage to Delphi, to ask how he could purify himself of guilt for his own children's blood, and so escape the avenging Furies.

Heracles took the mountain road, where eagles wheel overhead. At the last turn of the path he saw the valley of Delphi below him, a dark river of olives flowing to the sea. Here, men said, was the centre of the earth, its navel the stone Cronus vomited out at the beginning of time. Here Apollo gave counsel to men, through the mouth of his priestess, the Pythoness. Heracles went to her dark cave. She sat on a golden three-legged stool, a branch from Apollo's laurel tree in her hand, and drugged herself by chewing the sacred laurel leaves. She shuddered; the god was coming near. At last he possessed her wholly. She moaned and swayed in a trance, crying in a strange, high voice the words which were Apollo's message.

Often the god's words were hard to understand but to Heracles he spoke plainly. "Go to Tiryns, city of Perseus. There serve King Eurystheus for twelve years and do all the labours he commands."

To labour as a penance was often the way a man could free himself from blood guilt, yet Heracles would have chosen any master rather than this. He knew Eurystheus for they were both descended from Perseus, and, if Hera had not held back his birth by witchcraft, he would have been the first-born lord of Tiryns himself. Instead his cousin Eurystheus, a man as small in mind as body, was its tyrant. To serve him was shame of spirit, yet the gods must be obeyed. Sad at heart, Heracles went to await his orders. He set off over the great plain of Argos, towards Perseus's citadel. Iolus, the time of madness forgiven, went with his huge uncle, to carry his shield and spear. Some say the gods gave Heracles bronze shin-guards, a golden breast-plate and a plumed helmet, but he scorned to wear them. He carried his olive-tree club, and slung his hunter's bow across his back as he journeyed. The hare crouched trembling in her form as Heracles passed, shaking the earth with his giant strides.

Eurystheus first sent the hero to leafy Nemea, among the hills. Halfway up the hill, above a grove of poplars and a clear cold stream, still gapes the mouth of a cave. There lived a huge lion, with a hide that neither stone nor bronze could wound, which came out from its lair in the rocks to devour the countryside. Heracles was ordered to bring back this brute's hide. He lodged with the family of a labourer, whose son the lion had killed, and set out on foot. The country was clear and sharp in the morning light, the hillsides terraced under vine and olive, deep shadow in the valleys between. Not a soul was about, for many were dead and the rest hiding in terror.

Heracles searched all day in vain among the tumbled rocks. Then at evening the lion returned to its lair, tawny hide all spattered with spume and blood from the day's kill. Heracles crouched among the rocks and shot a flight of arrows. All fell broken from the iron pelt, while the lion lazily licked its chops. Then it sniffed the air and caught the scent of Heracles. The lion snarled and tossed its golden head, sharp teeth bared to rend and maim. With tail lashing angrily it gathered itself to spring.

Heracles crashed his tree-club upon the shaggy head. The tree splintered and fell from his hand, but the lion checked and shook itself, still dizzy from the blow. Then Heracles leapt on its back. Treading down its sinewy hindquarters, he locked his unconquerable arms in a wrestler's grip round its throat and squeezed until he felt the powerful body grow slack under him. He had strangled the lion with his bare hands. He cut the pelt with its own razor-sharp claws and flayed it. Then he slung the iron hide around him as a cloak, with the head as helmet, his own face looking out through the grim jaws. So armed he went back to Eurystheus. When the coward king saw a lion's skin

The Labours of Heracles—I

stride towards him, he ran away and jumped into a great brass pot for shelter. From that time on Eurystheus feared Heracles and always sent his orders by a herald.

The next labour was to go to a marsh, a spongy bed of moss, tall reeds and winding rivulets in the plain of Argos. There lurked a giant octopus, the Hydra, in her lair among the knotted roots of a plane tree. Heracles set off in a chariot, driven by young Iolus. As they reached the swamp, he loosed a flight of arrows, which brought the Hydra slithering from her hole in self defence. Holding his breath, he seized her, while slimy tentacles wrapped round his body. He hacked at them with a sickle, but wherever he cut one off, another grew in its place. Then a giant crab, the Hydra's servant, scuttled out of the swamp and seized his foot in ragged claws.

Heracles stamped on it angrily, and shouted for help to his nephew. From this comes the proverb you may still hear in Greece: "Even Heracles is done, in a fight of two to one." Iolus was a clever as well as a brave boy. Now he set fire to the swampy woodland; then, as Heracles slashed off the tentacles, Iolus seared each stump with a burning branch, so that no new ones could grow. As the throbbing tentacles fell away, Heracles worked towards the Hydra's head and plunged his dagger into the fatal spot between her eyes. Greek sailors still kill squids with the same stroke. Then Heracles hacked off the head, and flung it still hissing under the roots. He dipped his arrows in the Hydra's gall, and ever after, the least scratch from them brought instant death. As for the crab, many say that Hera had sent it, and that she put it among the signs of the Zodiac for a reward.

The next labour sounded easy, but was a cunning trap. Heracles was to capture a fallow deer, a swift dappled creature of rare beauty, with golden hooves and antlers. This woodland beast was sacred to Artemis, great goddess of hunting, who leads the chase through lonely glades. She would never forgive a man who hurt her beast, which shared her wild, free nature. So Heracles, for all his great strength, vowed to use no force. He stalked the deer for a whole year, without hounds or cruel traps, to the sea shore, where the distant islands shimmer in the heat, to the wild glens and the country beyond the north wind.

At last he found the deer sleeping in the shadow of a leafy dell; he bound her legs with gentle hands, and laid her on his shoulder, carrying her trembling to Mycenae. Artemis came to meet him, eyes flashing in anger. "Why do you seize the deer, which is my other self?" Heracles, tenderly holding the beast in huge, patient, grasp, answered "Lady of the beasts, because Zeus commands it." Even the goddess pitied him. She allowed him to carry the deer to Mycenae, where Heracles, kind as he was strong, let it go free.

The fourth labour sent him hunting again, this time in mid-winter. A fierce mountain boar was ravaging the pine-woods of Mount Erymantheus. He was ordered to bring back the brute alive; if he used too much force, he might kill it: too little and it might kill him. So Heracles dislodged the boar from its thickets with wild halloos and drove it up into the snow at the mountain peak. There the savage beast exhausted itself, floundering in the deep snow drifts. When its strength was spent, Heracles carried it back to the high hall where he flung it at the king's feet. Eurystheus fled in terror, vowing to plan some labour which would humble the hero's pride.

Nearby lived Augeas, king of Elis. No man in the world was so rich in flocks and herds. He had three hundred black bulls, two hundred red bulls and twelve sacred silver bulls, as well as thirty thousand cows. But Augeas had not cleaned out his cattle yards for thirty years; the pens were deep in sodden straw and dung, breeding fever in all the land, and the pastures so soaked in slurry that no grass could grow.

"Let him clean out the Augean stables," said Eurystheus with a grin, thinking of godlike Heracles, deep in the stinking dung. The hero went without pleading or complaint, and offered his services to Augeas, in return for a share of the herd. King Augeas laughed. "Swear to do it by nightfall!" he said as a joke. "I swear it by Zeus," said Heracles, the first and last oath he took in his father's name. He knocked two holes in the walls of the pen with his club, and dug trenches towards them from two mountain rivers.

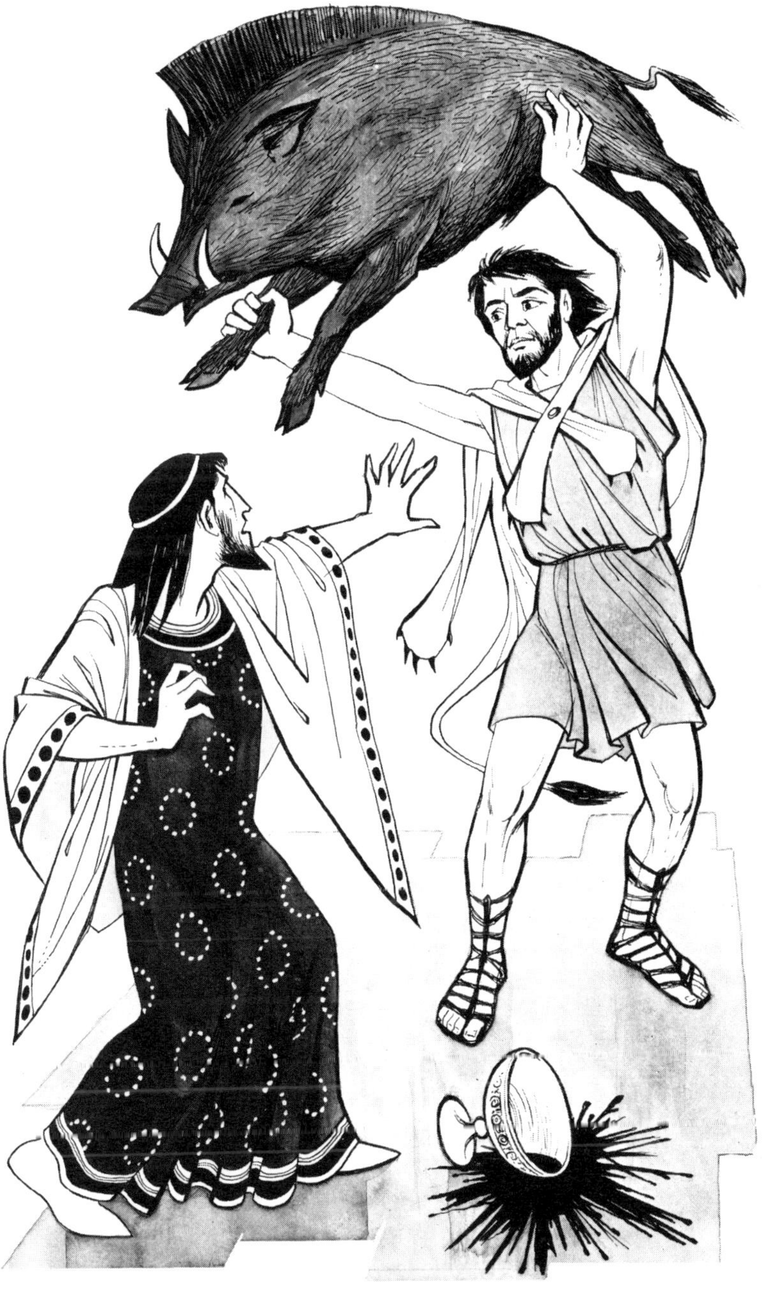

It was spring now. The high snows which had trapped the boar were melting in the sun's heat. The mountain streams rushed down in torrents banging their way from rocky ledge to ledge, thundering over waterfalls, sweeping everything before them. They surged through the filthy yards of King Augeas, scouring them clean and sweeping on, to stain the green sea brown far out from land. Heracles filled in the trenches again. By afternoon the yards lay empty and white, drying in the clear wind and sun. Heracles took his share of the cattle to buy land in order to found the great games at Olympia, pacing out the course himself with giant strides.

His next labour was again in a place of filth and sickness, a marsh haunted by birds with brazen claws and beaks, who spread malarial fever in their droppings. At first Heracles could not reach them, for the marsh was too soggy to walk upon, too muddy for a raft. Then Athena, mistress of skills, gave him a huge rattle of brass. He swung it with a hideous din, till the birds rose screeching in terror, and flew in a dense black cloud far beyond the seas, taking the marsh fever with them. Where men had shivered and burned with summer fire, where little children had drooped and died, a race of farmers grew their crops in the rich, dark soil.

So, in his first six labours, Heracles had freed the people of Greece from the fear of sickness and death. Now, bearing strength and courage as high gifts of the gods, he travelled to new labours in other lands.

The Labours of Heracles-II

FOR his seventh labour Eurystheus ordered Heracles to sail to Crete and capture a wild bull which was trampling the crops and overturning walls with the thrust of its mighty horns. No one even in that land of bull-fighters dared come near it, but Heracles caught it single-handed. He fettered it with leather thongs, carried it on board a boat, ferried it across the sea and drove it to Tiryns. Eurystheus, without sense or tact, offered the bull to Hera, who hated a gift honourably won by Heracles and promptly turned it loose. However the bull was now tamed.

Next, Heracles was sent far into the north, to Thrace, plain of swift horsemen. The whole land was in dread of four foul mares, kept by the King, Diomedes, and fed from bronze mangers upon human flesh. Heracles killed Diomedes in single combat and fed his body to the mares who tore at their master's body. At once these unbroken horses were tamed. Heracles put bridles over their heads, harnessed them to a chariot and drove them home four-in-hand.

For the ninth labour Heracles took ship again with a band of comrades and crossed the Black Sea to the windy plains of Scythia, land of superb Amazons. They were a tribe of fearless warrior women, swiftest of nomad horse-riders, first in the world to fight on horseback. Not for them the marriage feast or the friendly shout of neighbours' voices in the bride's song. Their bronze shields, shaped in a half moon, were sacred to the moon-goddess Artemis. Their holy place was a spreading beech tree, where they stamped the ground in wild war-dances to her glory. The Amazon girls wore tunics and caps of supple leather, and plaited their thick fair hair behind their backs, to leave the bow-arm free. They slept around their camp fires with the bare earth under them and feared no man living.

Heracles was commanded to bring back the sword belt of glorious Hippolyta, their queen. When he cast anchor upon the shore, he found the women-at-arms drawn up ready for battle. Vengeful Hera had gone about their camp in Amazon dress, whispering that the huge stranger would steal not the belt only, but the queen who wore it. The warrior women leapt on their horses and charged the ship. There was a hand-to-hand fight, with din of hooves, clash of swords, bronze-tongued battle yells and dust, shoulder high.

Most tellers of tales say Heracles captured the queen, and the sword-belt was the price of her freedom. Yet others tell that when Hippolyta saw the splendid body of the hero stripped for battle, she recognized a man worthy of her desire and gave him the girdle of her own free will, as a love token. Even an Amazon may feel the power of Aphrodite of the sudden glances. However it was, Heracles sailed home from the Amazons' land, his ship deep laden with metals and rich furs. Many say this was the birth of trade between Greece and the Black Sea shores.

Heracles had now explored all lands to the east and the north. His next two labours led him far into the west. On his journey westward he set up the Pillars of Heracles, two great rocks at the mouth of the Mediterranean Sea; these mark the limits of sailing and send adventurous men home to their own hearth fire. Beyond the Pillars roars the untrodden ocean, the limitless kingdom of Poseidon, the earth-shaker. In the western land of bitter orange-trees, lived a giant like a windmill, with three heads, three bodies joined together and six flailing arms. This giant kept a two-headed watchdog and a herd of splendid red cattle, in pastures facing the mysterious west. Heracles had to drive these cattle home to Greece without payment.

At the sight of him the watchdog cringed and shuddered. He killed it carelessly, with a passing blow from his club. Then he shot the giant, through all three bodies at once, with an arrow dipped in the Hydra's murderous gall. Next he drove the cattle home by slow stages through many lands. In summer he trudged along under the burning sun; on winter nights he drew the lion's pelt around him and fell asleep on icy mountain sides.

So he travelled painfully through Spain, through Gaul, through Italy and Sicily. Wherever he went, Heracles cleared the land of wild beasts, put down tyrants, forbade the heathen custom of human sacrifice, and gave the barbarous people good laws. So a new Greece grew up, a larger Greece beyond the seas. New cities claimed Heracles as their founder. Some worshipped him as a god.

All these labours had been done in the space of eight years and one month. Iolus, who had been a child when they set out, was now a young man, ready to take a wife. Even Heracles was weary, yet there were two more labours to do. The last but one was to find the apple tree of the singing and the gold. This grew beyond the sunset, where Apollo's golden horses fold their wings and finish their day's journey. There lies a garden, where the lovely daughters of Atlas sing under the evening star, as they circle round an apple tree with glittering golden fruit. These apples were earth's own wedding gift to Hera, a magic gift of fertility, too precious for man's hand to touch. A dragon guards them, tail of amber coiled around the tree trunk, scaly eyelids open night and day. This tree Heracles was ordered to strip, and bring the golden apples home. It seemed a task beyond the mind of man.

Heracles found the wisest counsel in the world, for during his travels he came upon the rock where Prometheus still lay in chains. Heracles, with heart as great as his strength, raged at such cruelty. His hands alone were strong enough to break the iron chains. He set Prometheus free and persuaded his father Zeus to forgive the age-old quarrel at last. In thankfulness Prometheus told him, "Go to my brother-Titan, Atlas. He alone can fetch the apples for you." Atlas, like a mountain, stood, feet on earth, back bowed under the crushing weight of the sky which he must hold up for ever.

"Help me to pick the golden apples," begged Heracles. "I would pick the apples," said Atlas wearily, "if you would hold up the sky—but no. It is too heavy for you." "Too heavy!" shouted Heracles, bending his huge back and raising his arms. In an instant Atlas had loaded the blue globe and the spinning stars on his shoulders and strode swiftly away. Planets whirled out of their courses and Heracles groaned before Atlas came back. In one large hand he held three golden apples, which the lovely singing nymphs of the sunset had gladly given him, since he was their father.

"I will take these apples to Eurystheus," said the Titan, stretching his aching back with sighs of relief. "Very well," said wily Heracles, "but let me first put a pad on my head, to soften the weight of the hard world." The great giant with the small brain took back his burden, while Heracles, giving him an ironical wave, picked up the apples and made off.

The powers of nature are strong, yet man's fearless hand and brain can master them. Heracles carried the golden apples home. But Athena, who judges all things wisely, took them back to the tree of life in the garden of the sunset where they belong, and no man has ever found that place beyond the western sea again.

One labour still remained, the last, the worst, the journey from which there is no return. Heracles was ordered to go down to the kingdom of Hades and bring back the hound Cerberus who guards the gate. He could not refuse, so he made ready for the journey. First he wisely prayed and sacrificed to Persephone, lady of the dead, at her altar. He washed his hands in pure water, sprinkled barley meal, took a black pig, Persephone's colour, and drawing back its head, cut its throat with one clean stroke of the knife. He burnt the

The Labours of Heracles—II

goddess's share on the altar and poured libations of blood and wine on the earth while the smoke rose upwards. Next he bathed in the river, to cleanse himself of all the blood he had been forced to shed during his labours. Then he was free to set out. Athena, who honours courage, walked with him unseen to guide his steps.

Heracles made his way through a maze of dark caverns on Cape Taenarum, where a steep shaft vanishes underground, and travellers are still shown his giant footprints. When he came to the black bank of the Styx, Charon the boatman took one look at the lion's pelt, the sharp claws and the set face of the hero looking out between the two rows of teeth. Miser though he was Charon rowed Heracles across without asking for his fare.

On the far bank Heracles found the ghosts of old friends and comrades waiting to greet him. "You have nothing to fear from us," they said sadly, for their souls without their bodies had neither strength nor will. Heracles poured an offering of blood, which gave them a brief life. For a while they talked over battles long ago and felt themselves almost men again. Then the king and queen of that dark country came out of their palace. Persephone, pleased by the sacrifice, smiled palely on Heracles, but her lord stood frowning by. "I demand your dog Cerberus," said the hero boldly. "He is yours," answered Hades, "if you can master him with your bare hands."

He smiled now, a smile of grim pleasure, for the dog Cerberus had three heads and a tail barbed to sting. Hades lets few who visit him go home again; and when fear comes from the gods even their sons run away. But Heracles would not run. He strode boldly to where the hound Cerberus strained snarling at his chain by the gate, ready to hunt down any dead soul who tried to slip back to the land of the living.

Then Heracles raised his bare, unconquerable hands and took the beast by the throat from which the three heads rose. The dog's tail lashed to sting him, but could not pierce the lion's hide. Heracles clenched throttling fists and would not loosen his grip till Cerberus half-dead foamed at the jaws, and yielded at last. Then he dragged him by the chain, barking furiously at the sight of green fields and sunshine, and tethered him at last by his own high gates.

Now the last of the labours was done and Heracles purified from the stain of his children's blood. In the long years of penance he had explored the world, freed it from dangers and sickness, founded new colonies for his country and made a better world for men. "Truly he is the son of Zeus," said the people, who all honoured him. "He rid us of the beasts, his labours gave us peace, and high above our birth his courage lifts him up." As for Heracles, who had laboured so long, he rested, tasted the honey of victory and found joy at last in labour's ending.

Heracles on Olympus

Now Heracles lived like a true prince of Mycenae, with feasting and shouting in his own high hall. All men honoured him, he fought many just battles, sacked tall cities and loved many women. But in the mid-summer of life he had still no wife or children of his own. After some years he went to ask for the hand of a beautiful girl, Deianira, daughter of the king of Calydon, who had many suitors. All the rest gave up promptly when huge Heracles appeared, except for Achelous, god of the greatest river in Greece. He stood his ground obstinately, streams of water trickling from his green and sedgy beard. "Take me as Deianira's husband," said Heracles to the king "and she will have Zeus himself for father-in-law." "At least," said Achelous with cutting disdain, "I have not been forced to labour like a slave." At this Heracles flared into one of his mighty rages. "I am better with my hands than with my tongue!" he shouted, and rushed upon his rival.

The river god slid out of his cold green cloak and they began to wrestle. It was an all-in fight with no holds barred, foot pressed against foot, arms locked, heads jammed together. Then Heracles broke free, streaming with sweat, and leapt on the god's back, with all his great weight. Slowly he forced Achelous to his knees and threw him face down in the dust. Achelous, who was not a god for nothing, deftly turned into a speckled serpent, and writhed away, hissing fiercely.

Heracles only laughed. "I strangled serpents in my cradle," he said, and locked his vast thumbs in a death grip round the snake's neck. Swiftly Achelous turned into a a bull, lowered his horns and charged. Lovely Deianira, the cause of the fight, looked on. "A bull for my husband!" she thought in horror, "a coiled, slimy snake, a river, seizing me round the waist with its cold arms! I would rather die. O all you gods, make Heracles win!"

Secretly she was already in love with the hero, as she watched him fight with bare, unconquerable hands. Now he seized the bellowing god-bull by the horns and forced its head slowly down, until the sharp ends were driven into the stony ground, and one horn snapped off. Achelous crawled away, angry and ashamed. Some even claim that Heracles drained his marshes making the river swamp into rich farm land. Meanwhile a wedding banquet was spread for Heracles and Deianira, when all feasted upon boar's flesh roasted with herbs, honey cakes and raisins.

After the feast, Heracles and his young bride set out for his own city. On the way they came to a flooded river, swirling and dimpling in eddies far over the land, as it carried the spring rains to the sea. Heracles flung his bow and arrows across in a mighty throw and made ready to swim, when he saw the girl was pale and trembling with fear. At that moment a centaur galloped up, one of those strange creatures from the high hills, with the head and trunk of a man rising from the body of a wild horse. "My name is Nessus," said the centaur courteously. "The gods have sent me to be your ferry-man. I will carry your fair wife across the flood, and set her safely on the farther bank, without even getting her feet wet." So Heracles lifted Deianira on to the centaur's back, and jumped into the stream himself, swimming strongly against the flood to the farther shore. But when Nessus felt the light weight of the lovely girl press on his back, a madness seized him. He thought only of her soft arms, her slender waist, her cloudy hair, and rearing on his hind legs, turned and set off at a gallop for his own cave in the hills.

Already they were almost half a mile away, the powerful hooves striking sparks from the stones, when Heracles heard his wife's screams and saw her disappearing in a cloud of dust. He snatched up his bow and poisoned arrows, took careful aim, and shot Nessus clean through the back till the barb came out of his chest. Dark blood spurted from both wounds, blood tainted with the deadly venom of the Hydra's gall. Nessus knew he must die. "I won't die unavenged," he muttered in his beard. To the shuddering Deianira he said aloud. "Take the blood from my wound, for it is a powerful love charm. Mix it with oil of the olive, rub Heracles's shirt with the mixture, and you may be sure he can never cease to love you." Deianira, a single-hearted girl and much in love, believed him. She collected the poisoned blood in a scent bottle, which she hid in the folds of her long dress.

Many years passed. The whole world heard of the great deeds of Heracles. Deianira was a happy and virtuous wife. Like all Greek girls, she had hung up her dolls in the Temple of Artemis when she married, to show she was now a woman, and brought a stick from her parents' hearthstone to light the sacred fire in her new home. She saw that her husband's courtyard and the rooms round it were well-swept, the cistern always filled with water. Strangers were welcome at her wide flung doors, to wash and eat and rest in the shade of her cool porch. She set the men slaves to work, filling the tall jars in her store-room with corn and olive, dried figs and home-trodden wine. The girls she taught to spin and weave at the loom, to tread the household washing in the river, and to bake good yellow barley-bread. The weapons hung well-polished on her walls and she swept the altars of the household gods with her own hands. Deianira was a good mother also, who bore Heracles four fine sons, tamers of horses, riders in chariots, winners in the foot race.

So all men pointed to Heracles's happy hall. But time goes wheeling on and the winds blow many ways. The loveliest girl becomes at last a jealous housewife. One summer, when the grasshopper sang in the burning heat from morning till night, Heracles sent home from war a young girl captive. A gossiping neighbour said he was in love with her. Some say this tale was true, some false; in any case Deianira believed it. "I see how it is," she said bitterly to herself. "Heracles's hand turns from the withered stalk and reaches towards the fresh new flower. He is my husband but her man." Then she thought of the scent bottle filled with Nessus's blood, which had lain all these years hidden among clean linen in a chest.

At this hour, for so fate willed it, Heracles sent a messenger to say he had captured a city and would offer thanksgiving to Zeus. He asked his wife to send a new shirt for him to wear when he prayed and sacrificed at the altar, as the ritual demanded. Deianira with her own hands wove a shirt of finest linen. Secretly she unsealed the bottle, soaked a tuft of wool in the blood and rubbed the shirt, believing still that this was a love philtre. She sent the shirt to Heracles with loving messages. After the servant had ridden off at a gallop, Deianira glanced down at the ground where she had dropped the wool and was terrified to see it burning like fire. She knew too late that Nessus had tricked her and cursed her own trusting heart.

Meanwhile on a high headland, Heracles had built his altar; he was going to offer the greatest of sacrifices, a hecatomb, in which a hundred offerings are burnt at once. The smoke, dissolving in the air, ascends to the gods on Mount Olympus, while on earth the worshippers feast together, with chanted prayers and music. Heracles put on the unworn shirt, kindled the fires and poured wine on the altar stones as he spoke the first prayer. Suddenly his flesh began to burn, as though a serpent had bitten him with venomous fangs; for the heat of the fire was melting the poison in the shirt.

Heracles bore the pain as long as he could in silence, but the Hydra's venom coursed through his veins, corroding the flesh. At last, with a terrible cry, he tore the shirt from his back, but it dragged the skin with it, laying bare the tortured flesh to the bone. Then Heracles raged like a madman, rushing over the mountain side and howling like a beast in his agony. Trees came crashing down in his path, dark sweat poured from his body, and the malignant fire within ate up his bones. As there had been no limit to Heracles's strength, so there was no limit to his suffering. His soldiers watching, saw him lift up his arms to the sky where Zeus his father lived, as though to ask, "Was it for this, all my toil and labour? Take away my life, O gods, for I can bear it no longer!"

Dark are the ways of gods to men. Until Heracles's labours were done his destiny preserved him, but now he was going down to the house of the dead. His soldiers built a funeral pyre of oak branches on the mountain top, and he lay down on it like a weary man ready for rest. Not one of his friends would light the fire, but a passing shepherd kindled it and Heracles gave him in gratitude the deadly bow and arrows. As the flames leapt up, Zeus sent a thunderbolt from heaven and in an instant mortal Heracles vanished from their eyes. When Deianira was told, she took a hunting knife from its peg on the wall and stabbed herself to death in their marriage bed.

As a snake casts its old skin, so Heracles cast off his toil-worn body and appeared, glorious, on Mount Olympus's shining floor.

He resembled his father Zeus, and so strange are the ways of goddesses and women, that Hera came to love him as her own son. For this reason he was given the name Heracles, Hera's glory. He became the porter of heaven and stands for ever at the shining gates of the sky, letting the immortals in and out. Faithful Iolus and his friends offered the first sacrifice in honour of Heracles and since then all Greece has worshipped him. "Greatly he suffered," wrote a poet, "but heaven-born joy brings grief itself to turn about with time." Young men pour yearly offerings of wine for him at sunset, sharing the libation with their friends. And when a boy's childish long curls are cut for the first time, he offers a lock at the altar of Heracles, bravest in battle.

Strange Journeys

The Girl on the Bull

THE gods from their shining floor can see all the doings of men upon earth. On a spring morning Zeus looked down through the blue air and saw Europa, daughter of King Agenor of Tyre, rich city of sailors and traders in purple dyes. Europa was walking to the sea shore with her maids, girls of age to be married, about fifteen years old. Swift and sure-footed as gazelles, the young girls chased the waves or filled their laps with flowers, while bright petals fell in a shower on the ground. Among them all Europa shone like a star and at the sight of her the heart of Zeus was troubled. His thunderbolts conquer giants and Titans, but even he cannot escape the spells of laughter-loving Aphrodite: she breaks the strength and overpowers the will of gods and men alike. Now, in love again, Zeus knew his shining glory would frighten the young princess, and resolved to visit earth in one of his many disguises.

At this very moment, the girls looked up from their play and saw a bull running towards them over the meadow. Their first thought was to cry for help and run away, but there was something about this bull which made them stop. They could see he was no common bull escaped from the farmer's pen, nor any kin to the oxen that drag his creeping cart. His body was noble, powerful-shouldered, his flanks glossy as silk. A silver circle shone between his brows; his horns were curved like two crescent moons and his great eyes gleamed so softly that the young girls could not fear him.

They gathered round him in wonder, they made garlands of flowers for his neck, they put their arms around him, and boldly stroked his silken flanks; but the bull had eyes for only one of them. He stood before the princess Europa and licked her hands and feet. When she stroked him, he murmured softly and his breath was sweet as summer meadows. At the touch of her soft hand he could hardly wait to possess her wholly. He bowed his head, arched his powerful neck, and showed her his back, looking up at her all the while with soft, shining eyes.

Europa clapped her hands. "Look, he is inviting us to ride on his back. Do let us go! I am sure he will not hurt us, for he is dear and gentle, not fierce like other bulls." She laughed with pleasure, and climbed boldly on his back, holding his horn with one hand, while the other patted his powerful neck. But now in a flash, before any of the others could mount, the bull leapt up and carrying Europa made swiftly for the sea. "Help me! Oh, help me!" cried Europa in terror. But the young girls could not reach her, and the bull raced swiftly over the sands to the water's edge, where it plunged like a dolphin into the sea. Europa dared not let go for fear of drowning. She rode on the back of the wonderful bull, while the salt wind filled her cloak. The watchers on the shore saw it, like a purple sail, the purple of her own land, carrying her over the water and away from them for ever.

Europa wondered at what she saw, for the wild sea grew smooth under the hooves of the bull, and sea monsters gambolled about them. Dolphins rolled and tumbled in their path, while scaly mermen rose from the waves, with conch shells at their lips blowing a bridal song. Europa looked all around her but there was no land to be seen. The last headland of her own country was left far behind, the scattered islands faint in the distance; there was only the glittering dark blue sea beneath her and the sky overhead.

Then she was afraid and began to cry. "Oh, who are you and where where are you taking me? You are not a bull; that I know, for you do not fear the sea, but run proudly over the water. You tread the waves and your hooves are not wet. Alas, I am sad for I know in my heart that I shall never see my father's house again!" Then the bull turned its head with the spreading horns and the eyes like two shining stars. "Be brave, beautiful Europa," it said. "Do not fear the salt waves or the hungry sea. I am Zeus, ruler of gods and men, to whom even the beasts of the sea do homage. I can change into whatever beast I will, and for love of you I put on this shape of a bull. Soon you shall be my bride and bear me glorious sons, kings among earthly men."

The bull ran on powerful and tireless, trampling the crested waves until the shores of Crete rose white before them. He gained the land and followed the track of a stony stream; you may still see the water brawl over the stones, and the sheep crop the wiry grass among the oleander trees. The stream led to a spring and a copse whose trees are always green, even in that thirsty southern land, a fitting place for love's rituals. All the god had spoken came to pass. Europa bore Zeus three sons, and the eldest, Minos, became king of Crete. He built a great palace, whose dark halls and secret stairs formed a labyrinth. His were the first people in the west to read, write, count and steer ships by the stars. They made wreaths and jewels of gold and covered their walls with bull paintings, in honour of the god who founded their nation. They were the first great rulers of the west, and called their lands Europe in memory of the girl on the bull.

The Winged Horse

THE land of Lycia was under a reign of terror. A mountain monster, the Chimaera breathing flame haunted its deep valleys, she had the head and the rending claws of a lion and the coiled tail of a serpent, to trap and bind her prey. Nothing was safe from her; she seized sheep, oxen, even young children, and carried them off to her lair in the mountains, where she devoured their raw flesh with hideous snarling. The peasants in the valleys, when they heard her roar, would whisper, "The Chimaera!" and clutch the charms they wore around their necks against the evil eye. In panic they drove the beasts into thorn-bush stockades and locked the children into their huts. Abandoned and neglected, the little fields lay white with thistles and the people starved. The lord of that land, Iobates, was sleepless with care.

Yet when a tall young stranger came from Argos, bearing letters from his daughter's husband, Iobates put aside his cares to give him a royal welcome. For nine days they feasted. Nine fat oxen were killed and roasted in the high hall, with flute-playing and dances. Then on the tenth day, he unwrapped the wax tablets and saw what was written there. "This man has tried to steal my wife, your daughter. Avenge the shame on both our houses; kill him." Iobates frowned and tapped the letter with a

The Winged Horse

thoughtful finger. He wanted to send the young man the shortest way out of the world, but guests are sacred. The avenging Furies hunt down the man who murders the stranger under his roof. Then a sudden thought struck him and he sent for his handsome guest, whose name was Bellerophon.

"Are you brave enough to free my poor country from the Chimaera?" he asked, with two-edged flattery. Bellerophon saw that the letter had been a plot to get rid of him. He had no hope of killing the monster, but he was young and proud. Destiny had planted glory in him, and dreams of godlike power. "What use," he thought, "is old age without a name?" So he held up his head and answered boldly: "Yes, I will."

That night, on the advice of a wise seer, Bellerophon went to sleep in the temple of Athena, bringer of good counsel. Moonlight flooded the colonnades in whiteness as he stretched himself on the stone floor, pillowed his head on his hunting-cloak, and fell asleep. It seemed to him that as he slept, someone came towards him in the moonlight, a woman, tall as the pillars of the temple, wearing a shining helmet and a breastplate of gold. "Do you sleep, Bellerophon?" she said. "You must wake and catch the winged horse, Pegasus, when he comes down to the fountain of the Muses to drink. Take this charm for a horse; lay it upon him and he will carry you safely to the Chimaera, though no man has ever ridden him before."

She laid by his side a bit and bridle of wrought gold, the first ever known on earth. Bellerophon saw that her sea-grey eyes shone with more than mortal wisdom and knew that Athena had come in his dreams to guide him. He woke at earliest dawn. A cold mountain wind blew through the open temple: mist wreathed the columns, the moon had sunk and with it the vision of the goddess. Yet, as he shook the sleep from his head and rubbed his numbed limbs awake, he found the golden bit and bridle, beside him on the ground.

He took the path to the fountain of the Muses, and hid with fast-beating heart among the rocks, the bridle clutched in both hands. It was a secret place, a hidden pool, now silent and deserted, where at evening the Muses sing with gold in their hair. He waited as the last dregs of night spilled from the sky.

At last he heard overhead the sweep of great wings. Shining in the morning light, the horse landed, folded its rustling wings quietly against its white flanks, and began to drink from its own reflection in the pool. Bellerophon stepped softly from his hiding place, but even before it saw him the beautiful creature scented man and shied away, its nostrils flaring alarm and its hooves striking sparks from the rocks.

"Pegasus," said the young hero softly, stepping towards it. "Pegasus, see, I have the horse-charm of the goddess." The power of the gods makes it easy to do what lies beyond our common hopes. The wisdom of the goddess, unseen beside him, taught Bellerophon what to do. He slipped the golden bridle over its head and the winged horse at once became quiet, lowering its head with schooled intelligence for Bellerophon to put the bit in its mouth. "To the lair of the Chimaera, Pegasus," he said and vaulted on its back. Then Bellerophon tasted glory indeed. The white wings unfurled like clouds below him, and their steady beat carried him up and up, soaring like a god into the sky, where the morning stars faded around him. "On, Pegasus, on!" he shouted like a god. The wind roared in his ears, his cloak streamed out behind him; gripping the powerful flanks with his knees, he sang aloud for joy and triumph. Around him lay all nature, within him the power of the gods.

Soon they came to the territory of the Chimaera. Bellerophon saw far below him fields of blackened corn and maize, scorched by her fiery breath. Indeed some have said the Chimaera was a mountain volcano, killing by rivers of fire, but this is not the tale the hero told. At the touch of his heel the winged horse flew lower, circling over the burnt-out land.

Suddenly Bellerophon gave a shout, for his sharp eyes had spotted the monster herself, crouched outside her lair. The Chimaera looked up at the sound of wings in the sky, saw the horse and rider above her, and roared in rage. A torrent of smoke, molten rock and crackling red flame burst from her open jaws. No mortal creature could have lived in that heat, but the godlike horse gathered its strength and swooped like Zeus's eagle. As they lunged through the sky, Bellerophon shot an arrow at the monster. A louder roar told him he had hit his

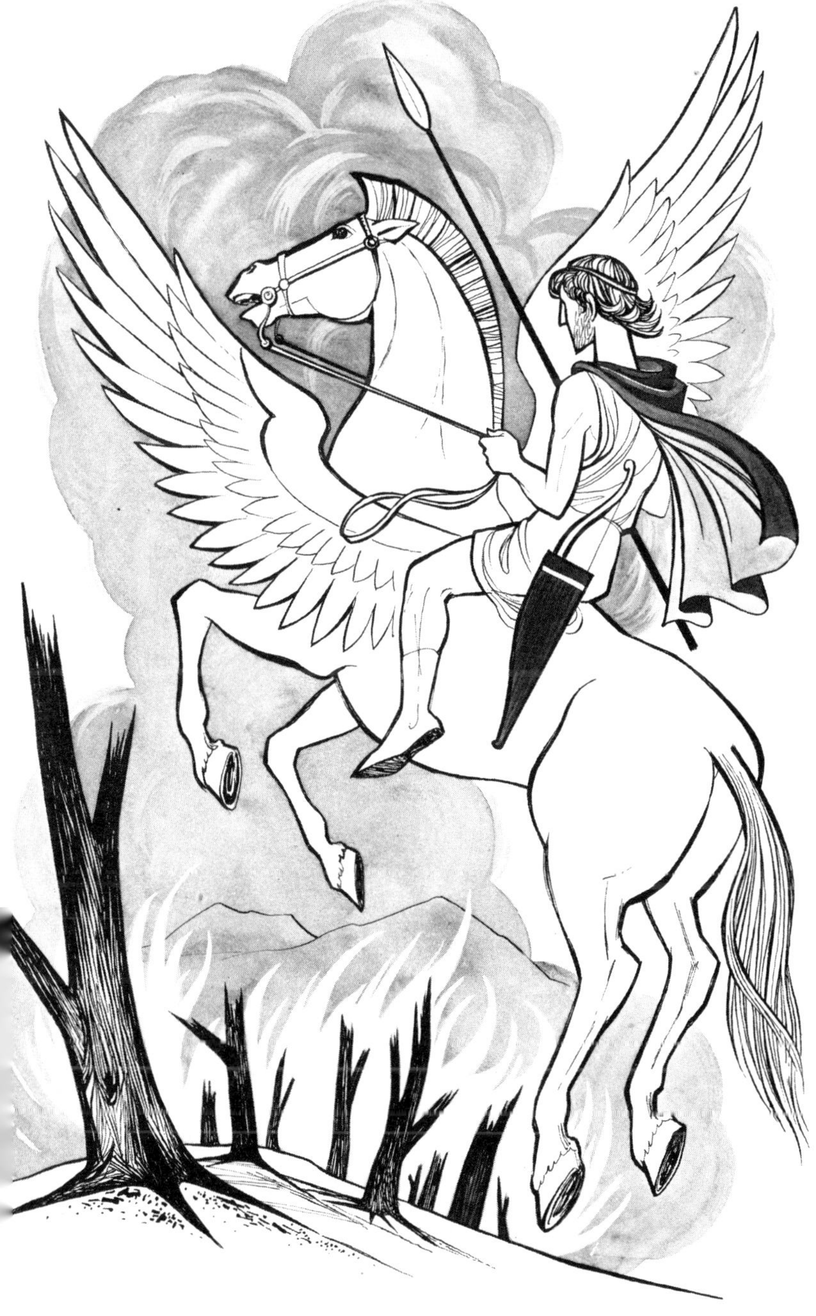

mark, but before he had time to see, Pegasus wheeled on the wing and climbed steeply out of the smoke and flames to the clear upper air. **Again and again they dived, riddling the** blood-flecked sides with arrows. Then Bellerophon poised his hunting spear, swooped again and thrust it with all the force of their fall into the Chimaera's jaws. The bronze melted in her red-hot breath, searing her lungs. She gave a last throttled roar, her serpent's tail lashed once, then dropped heavy and lifeless on the black earth. The mountain people of Lycia were freed for ever from the terror of the monster.

Iobates saw Bellerophon return in triumph astride his winged horse, with the Chimaera's head dragged in the dust behind them, and knew some god must have helped him. Bellerophon, with the help of Pegasus, overcame every enemy he was sent to fight, until at last Iobates gave him his favourite daughter in marriage and made him heir to the land of Lycia. So Bellerophon became rich and great and a ruler among men.

Yet the last years of his life were heavy with grief. The dream of glory which had made his youth shine in men's eyes betrayed him at last. For he forgot that it was by the help of the gods that he had triumphed and began to boast of his own cunning and bravery. "Seek not to become a god," runs the Greek saying; "mortal death is for mortal men." Bellerophon forgot this. He swore he would bestride Pegasus and fly to Olympus, to live in the sky's dwellings and feast for ever like an immortal in the company of Zeus. Man is too small to reach the bronze floor of the gods. When the gods heard Bellerophon boasting they held a council and planned a fitting punishment for their vainglorious favourite.

One morning, when Bellerophon leapt as usual on the back of his winged horse and soared up to gallop across the clouds, Zeus sent a gadfly to sting Pegasus. The horse, usually so obedient to every touch of rein or knee, grew wild with pain. Rearing and plunging in the sky, it hurled its rider from the saddle to the earth below, where Bellerophon ended his days a maimed, blind and lonely old man. As for Pegasus, he flew up to heaven and was stalled for ever in the stables of Zeus. You may hear the thunder of his hooves among the storm-clouds to this day.

The Man on a Dolphin

ARION was the greatest musician of his day; the men of Corinth where he lived boasted that he was the greatest since Orpheus. He composed immortal songs and harp music. When he played the lyre, singers and dancers were compelled to join in, as though the nine shining Muses led the dance. Arion had a desire to visit Sicily for a great music festival to be held in the Greek colony there. His friends on the mainland of Greece were sad to see him go.

They spoke of dangers from shipwreck or pirates, and how they could not bear to lose his genius, which was the city's glory. But no artist will be bound against his will. Arion insisted and took ship, promising to return soon.

He triumphed in Sicily. The sunlit curve of the theatre in the hillside was hushed to hear him sing; afterwards thousands of voices cheered together. He took all the first prizes in the festival and the judges crowned him with Apollo's sacred laurel, more precious to a musician than fine gold. Arion grew rich also. Admirers showered him with gold coins, rings, buckles, wreaths of delicate gold leaves, robes and rich furs from far-off northern lands. After some days and nights of feasting, he remembered his promise to his friends in Corinth and said he must go home.

Arion took ship on the regular service from the port of

Syracuse to Greece. The ship was like all the other Greek ships, coming and going among the islands, small, but sturdily built, curved like the crescent moon to ride rough water. In the well amidships, open to wind and spray, sat the rowing slaves, a wretched gang of prisoners and captives. When the winds were contrary they pulled on heavy oaken oars; when the wind swung behind them, the captain would shout to step the mast and rig the one square sail, held taut by creaking ropes.

The passengers lay aft, with an awning to shelter them from rain or sun. Arion, a seasoned traveller, like all musicians who must go on tour, saw his baggage safely aboard. Sailors, stripped to the waist, sweated up the gangplank, with his new boxes, baskets, bales of cloth, chests of coins and jewels. The captain stood on his bridge forward, a man thin and hard as a bronze coin, with shrewd glances and few words. "A rich passenger," he thought to himself, but waited his time. He looked, as seafaring men do, for the luck of the wind. Satisfied, he shouted the order to cast off and the slaves dragged on their oars. Within an hour they were so far out to sea they no longer saw the sunlight flash from the golden shield of Athena on the temple roof. Around them in splendour rolled Poseidon's kingdom, the unharvested sea.

The voyage passed idly for Arion, as sea voyages do. Mast and cordage creaked overhead. Sometimes the wind shifted a point and the sail flapped lazily. He lay in the sun, ate oftener than he needed, to pass the time, and slept away the noonday heat. When cool evening came he sat on a coil of rope and looked out over the sea. The waves shone darkly blue, islands in the distance seemed to slide past with astonishing speed and the sails of passing fishermen dwindled to nothing at the line where sky and sea meet.

The day's heat dissolved at last in violet mist. Then music stirred in Arion's being. He fetched his lyre and played, while the sailors, arms linked in one long line, danced barefoot on the deck. Even dolphins and shy seals yielded to the spell of his music. They followed the ship in shoals, black heads bobbing above the water, lithe backs rippling in delight. But when night came the sailors crawled into their hole under the foredeck and whispered greedily about their rich passenger.

The Man on a Dolphin

When they were some days out from land, the captain of the ship came to Arion with that barbed courtesy in which all Greeks delight. "We much regret, Arion, that you will have to die," he remarked. "Why, what crime have I committed?" asked Arion. "You are too rich," answered the captain, with a flash of white teeth. "Spare my life," pleaded Arion, "and I promise to give you all my prizes." "No doubt," said the captain. "But would you keep your promise when we get to Corinth? In your shoes, I for one would not." There was no island, no ship in sight, nothing but limitless sky and sea. Arion, seeing that further words were useless, made up his mind to die like a man. "I am resigned," he said, "but at least let me make an end worthy of an artist." The captain, respecting such courage, gave his permission.

Then Arion put on the finest of his ritual robes: a tunic of fine pleated linen, a purple cloak such as Apollo wears, and on his head the sacred laurel wreath which marks a follower of the god. He tuned his lyre for the last time, with listening ear intent upon the seven strings. Then he stepped proudly on to the captain's bridge and began to play with such passion that even the ruffian crew fell silent. Around the ship the seals and dolphins circled, spellbound by the music. With one last heart-breaking cadence, Arion, lyre in hand, flung himself overboard, to meet death proudly of his own free will. The ship sailed on and all believed him drowned. Greedy and quarrelsome as starlings, they divided his possessions.

No one saw a splendid dolphin swim up as though Arion had called it, dipping in the trough of the waves and mutely inviting him to mount its back. Arion scrambled astride the powerful fish, gripping its sides with his knees, while the dolphin blew sea fountains through its nostrils like a flourish of trumpets to clear the way. He could hardly remember what followed. Was it a dream, the marvellous sea-ride, the great creature leaping and plunging under him through the clear sea waves, the salt in his nostrils, the sea-wind in his hair? Arion felt like a god, while all the time the powerful fins thrashed the water, carrying him towards Corinth.

They made landfall that night. Arion's friends were overjoyed at the miracle of his escape. He could not bear to part from the dolphin, but took it to his house, where it lived in a fish pond. A few days later the ship docked. The ruler of the city at once sent for the captain and crew, whom he asked with pretended anxiety about their famous passenger. "Alas!" replied the captain, with one of his too-ready smiles, "the great Arion did not sail with us after all. He was detained in Sicily by his many admirers. Indeed, I am doubtful whether he will ever return." The ruler made them swear to this, then confronted them with Arion face to face. The villains broke down, confessed their guilt, and were executed on the spot.

As for the dolphin, it became the darling of high society. The great and famous crowded to see how it came at its master's call and gambolled in the water. They flung it titbits of rich and unaccustomed food from their own banquets. They did not understand the law by which each creature must live true to its own nature. Thinking to praise the dolphin they destroyed it, for the marvellous intelligent creature died of this unnatural life. Arion gave it a lordly funeral. Later he went out to the temple of Poseidon, whose columns bleached by sun and air rise on a headland, high above the sea. He first poured oil and wine on the waters as an offering, then took up his lyre to sing. Later he wrote this down on tablets of wax, which unhappily were broken. Yet from fragments remaining, we believe that this, or something like it, was his song of thanksgiving.

> Poseidon, Lord of the waters,
> Be praised by all creatures within,
> Seals from their cavernous quarters,
> Oceans of shimmering fin.
> Dolphin the chief, whose true
> Intelligence rescued a singer
> From peril, bearing him through
> Safely to land, the home-bringer.
> When human greed had consigned me
> A cruel sea grave, you it was,
> Dolphin, followed to find me.
> You above all let me praise!

The Flying Ram

THE young prince Phrixus and his sister Helle were children of Athamas, king of Thebes. Thebes was a mighty fortress, its men lovers of glory with hearts above possessions, but so many tragedies befell them that people said there must be a curse on the city. Its founding had been magical.

When Europa was stolen by the bull-Zeus, her brother Cadmus set out to search for her. On his travels he killed a dragon, its huge mouth bristling with murderous teeth. Cadmus, advised by Athena, pulled out the teeth and scattered them on the ground like seed corn. A crop of armed warriors sprang up. They fought each other until all but five were dead, and with these five Cadmus founded the new city of Thebes.

They built a citadel with seven gates, and massive stone walls, which the Thebans defended through many wars and sieges. Cadmus taught his people their first alphabet of sixteen letters, and Zeus gave him a goddess as wife. She brought with her a lovely necklace of wrought gold, the wedding-present of the gods. Alas, it proved a fatal gift, for, as this story will tell, it brought ruin to every woman who clasped it round her neck.

Phrixus and Helle grew up in the great citadel of Thebes. There, within the huge walls, rock thrusts through the wiry grass; the air smells of thyme and goat-droppings. It is open to the four winds and the sky, and the two children grew up strong and free. Their parents, though, were not happy in marriage. Their father was a warrior who loved the shout of battle and feasting, their mother a silent woman who loved to wander alone over the hills. Her name was Nephele, the Cloud, and many believed she had been made by Zeus from the clouds that float overhead. At last she vanished entirely. Her son and daughter were left as though motherless, to be cared for by the slaves and captive women of the palace. The king their father lost no time, but married again, this time a woman all too surely of flesh and blood. Ino was a daughter of Cadmus and inherited from her mother the sumptuous golden necklace which brought ruin to its wearer.

To Ino it brought jealousy, destroyer of love and layer-waste of lives. Ino was beautiful, her husband loved her and she had children of her own, but none of these gifts of the gods gave her joy. She hated her two step-children, Phrixus and little Helle, for their place in their father's heart. To see them grow, handsome and beloved, was grief to her. Their kindness, their clear intelligence, seemed to threaten her peace. Degraded by torturing jealousy, she could not wait to be rid of them, not daring to kill them herself, for fear of their father, but plotting against them secretly day and night. At last her restless mind formed a plan.

Ino went by night and stole the seed-corn which was kept in the temple of the Mother Demeter for next year's sowing, corn sacred as the buried Daughter Persephone herself. Ino pretended to her waiting women that she knew a charm to make this seed bear heavier ears of wheat. At her command her women lit a brazier of charcoal in her innermost sleeping-room. Then Ino took a bronze shovel, heated it red hot and threw into it the city's future food. The grains hissed and sizzled over the fire, while the living germ of wheat in them was destroyed for ever. Then Ino returned the corn, to the temple and watched, saying nothing when the priests scattered it over

The Flying Ram

the winter fields with prayers and offerings. So hateful jealousy walks with fair words, but plots death. The winter frosts broke the ground, the rainy months passed, but no green shoots thrust through the earth.

Famine seized the city of Thebes. The corn jars were empty; the women went wailing about the dusty streets, saying the Mother had locked up the earth in anger. Then Ino spoke with a honeyed voice to her husband. "Send messengers to Delphi, to learn from the priestess who it is has angered the gods." When the messengers were chosen, Ino called them to her secret room and stripped the bracelets and gold chains she was wearing. "These are yours," she told them "if you will say that Demeter demands Phrixus as a sin-offering, before she will unbind the earth." The messengers returned with this pretended message, and for a little while the sad, ugly heart of Ino knew hope. "You cannot put your son's life before your starving people," she urged her husband. "Kill Phrixus at the altar and your corn will grow again." The king wrung his hands and wept loudly, but saw no escape.

Weeping, his father led Phrixus to the mountain top, where the priest waited, while slaves built a fire of brushwood to burn the chosen victim. Ino followed leading her sons; some say she had dressed them in white, and put black clothes on her step-children. There on the high place stood the sacrificer with the knife, the king full of sorrow and Ino full of dreadful joy. Phrixus grown almost to manhood stood waiting like a hero, as though glory not death were in his grasp. Suddenly a voice spoke through a cloud. "My children," said Nephele from empty air, "though you cannot see me, I watch over you. Hear your mother, and ride on this sacred beast to safety."

As they gazed up in wonder, the cloud parted and a ram flew down. He was no ordinary leader of a shepherd's flock, but a god among beasts. His hooves trod the earth delicately, as though they could think for themselves, his eyes shone with a pure light, his noble head was crowned with a pair of spiralling horns. His fleece was of soft shimmering wool, bright gold like a cloud in the sunrise; its soft rays gilded the earth where he stood. This glorious beast knelt down at the feet of Phrixus and spoke. "Climb on my back," it ordered. Phrixus swung a leg across its broad withers, compelled like a man in a dream. Suddenly he heard a child cry. "Oh, take me too," sobbed his sister Helle, "for I am afraid of our step-mother!" Phrixus reached out an arm and caught up the little girl, setting her on the ram's back behind him, where she sank in the soft golden wool of its fleece. Instantly the ram rose to its feet and flew up into the sky, vanishing among the clouds with Phrixus and Helle. Soon the watchers on the hill-top could see them no more.

Then the king grew mad with grief and rage. He seized Ino's eldest son and dashed him to pieces upon the rocks. Ino snatched up her younger child and fled for her life. She ran until she came to a cliff-top that overhangs the sea. There she flung herself into the water, the child still in her arms, and dissolved in foam. Even now she knows no peace, but is restlessly tossed to and fro on the waves. You may see her still on the water, still wringing her long white hands. So a woman's jealousy destroyed a whole family.

All this time the golden ram flew strongly towards the east, with Phrixus and Helle on its back. The coloured countries and the sea, thick sown with islands and ships, were drawn away like a carpet beneath their feet. All around them were shining air and white clouds sailing. Phrixus felt possessed by powers of nature, beyond him yet within himself; Helle as though in a dream clung round her strong brother's waist.

The day went down in flames behind them, while night rose to meet and cover them from the east. On through the violet darkness sped the flying ram: watchers on earth looked up and saw it pass, like a tailed comet or a shooting star across the sky. Phrixus was wide awake with joy and daring, but when night came little Helle felt a longing to sleep. The wheeling stars so near and so brilliant made her giddy; her heavy eyelids closed and she remembered no more. Slowly her loosening arms slid from her brother's waist and she dropped peacefully, without waking, into the sea. The sea nymphs took the sleeping child into their soft arms, rocking her to and fro on the waves like a cradle. Even today the narrow sea between Europe and Asia is called Helle's bridge, the Helle's pont.

The ram flew on with Phrixus, as the world slowly turned and morning came up from the east to meet them. Then like an eagle with long swoop from afar, it glided down and landed in the kingdom of Colchis in Asia minor. Phrixus looked around him, rubbing tired eyes. They were on an open green by the shores of the Black Sea, surrounded by a forest of oak trees. The ram bent its weary knees to kneel; then it spoke again. "Phrixus," it said, "Zeus, the protector of those who flee for their lives, has saved you. Build an altar here, and offer me as your sacrifice of thanksgiving."

Phrixus hesitated; he was young and the ram was his friend. The godlike beast seemed to read his thoughts and answered calmly: "I know if you kill me that it will not be in cruelty or ingratitude. Take my life, and I shall never be sold, or shorn of my golden fleece, never grow old and weary like other beasts. I shall be happy for ever in the shining fields of Olympus." So Phrixus drove his sharp knife deep into the ram's throat; a swift, clean killing, without pain or fear. He flayed it, built an altar of stones around a black rock, lit a wood fire and burnt its body as a sacrifice. The power of the ram drifted upwards in smoke to the gods. Phrixus hung its golden fleece on an oak tree.

The wood was ever after sacred and the gods sent a never-sleeping dragon to coil itself round the tree and guard the golden fleece. Phrixus was welcomed by the king of Colchis as a worker of wonders and favourite of Zeus. Because he had brought the golden fleece he was given the king's daughter in marriage, without paying the usual bride-price. He grew rich and famous. His house-doors stood wide to welcome strangers. When he died he was buried with honour, and the golden fleece still hung, lighting up the dark wood. To the Greeks it was a magical treasure at the world's end, a beacon to all adventurers.

*Two Heroes
who were Mortal*

The Man with one Understanding

JASON'S father was the king of Thessaly, in the north of Greece. He and his vast flocks lived in the wide plain beside the sea and his sailing ships rode in the bay called the gulf of Pegasus. But a scheming cousin, Pelias, stole the kingdom by force for himself. He even threatened to kill the new-born boy who was rightful heir to the throne. The palace women outwitted this murderer. They darkened the house, tore their clothes and wailed loudly, pretending the baby had been stillborn. Then secretly, they wrapped the child in purple swaddling clothes, to show he was a prince, and smuggled him away to the hills. Only night knew the secret of their road.

The boy grew up in the high hills, in the cave of Chiron, the centaur, open to the vast blue air. He learned to ride bareback, grasping the centaur's rough horse-body between his naked knees, while he listened to all its wise old man-body could teach him. All the princes of Greece sent their sons to Chiron for schooling.

Chief among the boys in the cave was Asclepius the good physician, who, some men said, was Apollo's true son. In that wild hill country Asclepius learnt respect for life: carrying lambs to safety out of the snow, watching the snake cast its old skin, and the wild mares drop their foals in the heather. He learnt the shepherds' craft of setting broken bones by touch, and found the herbs which calm fever, not by barbarian magic, but by thought and care. So he grew skilled to cure men and women whose bodies were wounded by bronze, or wasting with summer fire, taking their sufferings upon himself and waiting with steady patience for the healing time. All who came to him, Asclepius, the servant of nature, delivered. His followers took as their emblem the snake which renews itself and have ever after been physicians from father to son.

This good schooling the royal boy from Thessaly shared, and Chiron gave him the name of Jason, the Healer. Jason lived twenty years in the centaur's cave, sharing all things in freedom with his friends. In all that time he did nothing to be ashamed of. Above all, he learnt, so he was fit to teach. These years were a troubled time for Pelias, who feared the punishment of the gods. He went to Delphi, the place of the great stone which Chronos had vomited out at the beginning of time.

There, in the dark cave of the oracle, he asked the entranced priestess if he were safe in his stolen kingdom. She answered, as so often, in words that were a riddle: "Beware at all costs of the man with one understanding, when he comes from the hills to the sunny plains of Thessaly." This saying haunted Pelias, chilling his pale heart, though he could not fathom what it meant. The twenty years that passed so fast for Jason in the centaur's cave crawled their weary length in the troubled palace of the king.

In time a stranger came to Thessaly. He appeared in the market-place where people gathered to buy and sell their farm-produce, and his appearance set all the market women talking. He was fair-haired, like the men of the north, tall and proud of bearing. His hair had not been cut, but flamed in bright locks down his back. He wore a close-fitting leather tunic, revealing his splendid body. A leopard-skin cloak was flung over his shoulder and he wore one sandal; the other foot was bare. Now Pelias drove up in his bronze chariot and saw the young stranger. His guilty heart stood still with fear, for a man with one shoe is a man with one "under-standing". At last he knew the meaning of the oracle's words.

To hide his fear, the king spoke roughly and rudely. "What's your name, and what dirty ditch were you born in?". The young man showed his good schooling, for he answered the vulgar insult without anger. "Chiron was my schoolmaster and he called me Jason." "Why do you come here with only one shoe?" asked Pelias urgently. Jason answered. "I came to a river ford on the road, and a poor, lame old woman asked me to help her across. Carrying her on my back, I lost a sandal in the river mud." Jason did not know the black-shawled old hag had been Hera of the golden sandals, who was ever after his powerful helper and friend.

Pelias glared balefully at Jason, wishing him dead, and asked, "What do you want in this place?" "Only what is mine by right," answered the young man calmly. "I am the true king's son, and I have come to claim the throne of my father, which I am told crafty Pelias stole by force." Pelias drew himself up in his glittering chariot, behind his proud horses. "I am Pelias," he said, accustomed to strike terror with one frown. Yet the young man remained as civil as ever. "We often choose by greed instead of by what is right," he said, "but next day we find the choice tastes bitter in our mouths."

Pelias, grinding his teeth in rage, could think of no answer, and Jason continued easily. "We two are of one blood and should not fight our own kith and kin. Keep your sheep and red oxen, keep the palace and pastures you stole from my father, if possessions mean so much to you. They mean nothing to me. But give me the throne which is mine by right, to sit in judgement before my tribes of fearless horsemen. Do this and no fresh evil will come between us." These words, so quietly spoken, were none the less a threat. Jason had an air of mastery, hard to resist.

The mind of Pelias twisted and turned like a weasel in a burrow, to find a way out. At last he said, "I will do as you say, for I am at the withered end of life, while your youth is just bursting into leaf. But first free our country from a curse. The ghost of Phrixus haunts it, calling us to fetch home the fleece of the golden ram which carried him over the seas. When this is done, I swear you shall be sole ruler and king; let Zeus be the witness, the Thunderer who is lord of us both." Jason knew this was a trap, for the quest of the golden fleece in the distant land of Colchis was a long and dangerous one. But the old man and the young clapped hands in a bargain and swore an oath before Zeus. Pelias hoped in his secret heart that Jason would never see home again.

Then Jason ordered a ship from a master-craftsman, who built the *Argo*, the first long ship to sail the Mediterranean Sea. Athena, mistress of all skills, gave the ship's stem, a great beam from a grove of sacred oak trees. This magic beam had a voice which could speak to the crew, the voice of the *Argo* herself. The maker hewed long timbers and laid them in rows on the beach to take up salt water, while he shaped wooden bolts and bolt-holes. *Argo*'s sides were curved like the crescent moon and tarred against foul weather; her tall mast was a trimmed fir tree, and her painted sail was made fast with stout ropes of cactus fibre. There were fifty oars, and room on the benches amidships for fifty men to row, if the wind swung against them.

Then Jason sent heralds through all the cities of Greece asking for volunteers to go with him on this great adventure. Hera, who had not forgotten Jason, filled the hearts of all the young men in the land with longing for the good ship *Argo* and the golden fleece. Not one wanted to stay home safely with his mother; even if they died, they longed to share the joy of adventure with friends as young as themselves. So they flocked to the port, where the *Argo* waited in dry dock, on tree-trunk rollers, for her launching.

Jason welcomed them all. Never before or since did a ship have such a gallant company. Each brought some special strength or skill to the voyage. There was Tiphys, who knew the winds and stars by heart, as steersman, and Lynceus, so sharp-sighted he could see through solid earth, as a super-lookout. There was the builder of the *Argo* for repairs, with a useful friend who could walk on water. There was bookish Mopsus, who understood the language of beasts. There were

The Man with one Understanding

the sons of the founders of Greek cities and the fathers of the future heroes in the Trojan war. There was mighty Heracles with his young page, and Orpheus to play to them on the journey.

There were also the immortals: two sons of Hermes, with their father's charm and tact, two sons of the north wind with scarlet plumage ruffling at their backs, and twin sons of Zeus, one a jockey and one a champion boxer. The leader of this strong team was Jason, whom they elected captain of the ship. The whole crew together were called the Argonauts, the *Argo*'s sailors. "Great Zeus!" exclaimed a townsman, who saw them stowing their boat gear, "If the king of Colchis won't give them the fleece, this lot will send up his palace in smoke the day they get there!" Yet it was to happen, by a private joke of laughter-loving Aphrodite, that all these muscular heroes could not capture the fleece without the help of a young girl.

The Argonauts stowed gear and stores under the benches, hauled the bronze anchor aboard and shipped the oars. Then Tiphys shouted the order. With a mighty heave the young men sent the *Argo* running down the log rollers and launched her with a loud splash in the sea. They were ready to embark, but first they piled up stones to build an altar on the shore to Apollo, god of departures. Soon a fire of olive wood crackled. Jason sprinkled holy water and barleycorns and poured an offering of wine on the shingle. Heracles killed an ox, and they burnt the sacred portion, watching the smoke go up in dark spirals with their prayers, to the home of the gods above. "Lord, give me luck as I cast off," prayed Jason. "May there be kind weather and may I return bringing the golden fleece." The ship creaked and groaned in the water, the sacred oak beam crying out aloud to be off and away.

The Argonauts climbed aboard to their agreed places on the rowing benches. They struck the waves with their oars in time with the music of Orpheus. It was as though they were dancing together, their strokes kept such perfect time, while the salt foam surged round the blades. Out they struck strongly, to the open sea, their sharp keel cutting the water and a long, white wake, rippling behind them. Once out of harbour, they unfurled the sail and hauled it taut, seeing the wind fill it and hearing a shrill singing in the shrouds as it drove them swiftly on.

The watchers on the shore saw them dwindle to a speck between sky and sea. Old Chiron their schoolmaster had come down to see them off. As long as he could see, he waved one great arm, while the other carried a little boy, Achilles, who would grow up to fight at Troy. The aged priestess of the city had come down too, meaning to bless Jason, but had not even been able to speak to him in the jostling crowd. Now she was left behind, to watch him out of sight, as the old are always left by the young. And the wind of heaven drove *Argo* on her way.

The Voyage of the 'Argo'

JASON was aiming for the end of the known world, the far shore of the Black Sea. Its waters were so treacherous that men called it in whispers the Unwelcoming Sea, though out loud they said the Welcoming Sea, for fear of offending it. The Argonauts had many adventures on the way when each played the part Fate had written for him. One man had this skill and one that, but all were joined in friendship, and to help one another in need is friendship's highest joy. Only handsome Jason, the captain, sometimes wondered what purpose he served on the journey. Destiny waited for him, but his time had not yet come.

For their first landfall, the Argonauts came to an island where the women had rebelled and slaughtered every man. The angry women came down to the beach wearing their dead husbands' armour and ready to fight; but the two sons of Hermes, with all their father's engaging charm, persuaded the militant women to give them one night's shelter. The one night became many nights, for Aphrodite the creator of new life will not be denied. The women all fell in love with the young heroes and would not let them go. They feasted and danced, welcomed them to their beds and bore a whole new generation of children.

After many months Heracles at last growled, "Are we here to find the golden fleece, or to repopulate this island?" After that, not a man could look him in the face for shame. They hastily took to their boat again, while the women waved goodbye, with tears and prayers for the handsome young lovers they were losing. To this day the people of that island proudly claim descent from the Argonauts.

Now for many days the ship's company rowed by day, and slept by night in rocky island harbours, or on pine-scented beaches. The king of Troy guarded the narrow Hellespont where Helle had fallen, and let no Greek ships pass. But by night the Argonauts slipped through, hugging the coast, until they entered the darkly swirling waters of the Sea of Marmora. Here they came to Bear Island, home of a terrifying tribe of giants. At first sight they seemed to have six arms, for they wore bear-skin cloaks, with four whirling paws still hanging from each pelt. These savages rushed down their mountain, hurling jagged rocks at the Argonauts and trying to block the harbour mouth behind them. But Heracles quickly rallied the Argonauts, calling them to shoot, as he bent his bow and loosed his deadly arrows. In the end all the giants of Bear Island were killed.

Next the Argonauts had a grievous adventure. The north wind got up against them in the night, and drove them back with gale force. They scudded round in circles until they were driven on the shores of Cyzicus, where the king had already welcomed them kindly. In the dark, and through the shrieking wind, no one had the sense to know where they were, and the king, taking them for pirates, led his army out to fight them. There was a clash of spears and shields by night, each man hitting out wildly and blindly in the dark. Jason killed the friendly king, shattering his breast bone with one thrust. The Argonauts laid about them with battle yells, and drove the broken army back. In panic the defenders made a wild rush for their own city gates. Then came the morning, with a cold, livid sky. The Argonauts saw their cruel mistake, with the good king who had been their friend lying dead in dust and blood. For three full days they mourned him, wailing and tearing their

The Voyage of the 'Argo'

clothes as though he had been one of their own comrades. Then they and his own people gave him a chieftain's burial. The long barrow which is his grave stands on that lonely shore to this day.

As though to avenge this good king's blood, the Argonauts had foul weather which held them prisoner night and day for the next twelve days. On the thirteenth day a halcyon, the sea-bird which loves calm weather, hovered above Jason's head and perched twittering on the *Argo*'s prow. Mopsus, who understood the language of birds, told them its message. They should sacrifice to the Earth Mother on Bear Mountain, when the wind would drop. So they carved a rough image of the first great goddess, poured wine on the blazing sacrifice and danced before the altar, to the music of their clashing swords and shields. True enough, as the bird had promised, the wind dropped, and they rowed away through glassy, halcyon days.

After a long passage through the Sea of Marmora, they came to an island, and drove the *Argo* with grinding keel on to the beach. As usual all worked together to pitch camp. Some went to find dry wood, while others struck flint sparks to kindle a fire. Others heaped up dry leaves for bedding, while Hermes's two diplomatic sons went to trade with the islanders for a sheep to roast over the flames. Heracles' young page, well trained by his master, set off by moonlight with a bronze jug to look for drinking water. Presently he came to a clear spring. The nymph of the fountain saw this young mortal and her heart was flooded with desire. As he bent over the spring, she slid her cool arms round his neck and softly, with smiles and sidelong glances, drew him into the depths of the pool. There he has lived with her ever since.

When the boy did not come back, Heracles who loved him set off in search. He plunged frantically through the woods, beating the undergrowth till the sweat poured off him. He searched all night until the morning star appeared, bringing a favourable breeze. The Argonauts shouted for Heracles and his page till the hillsides rang, but there was no reply. At last, since the steersman urged it, they shook out sail and were driven far out to sea, leaving the wooded island on their bow. The boy was never seen again and Heracles, at last turned homewards with giant strides, heavy of foot and heart alike.

The Argonauts, usually such good friends, almost quarrelled about leaving him behind, but a merman thrust his green head through the swirling foam and blew his shell horn, telling them to sail on with no regrets, for such was the will of Zeus. Then the wind swept the *Argo* steadily onwards, her crew united in friendship once more.

Next they put in at an island where the tribal chief was a bully who fancied himself as a heavy-weight boxer and challenged all strangers to a bout. Any who refused he hurled over a cliff; indeed he had been the death of many travellers. When he bellowed his usual challenge to the Argonauts, the boxer son of Zeus coolly stripped off his clothes and pulled on the raw-hide boxing gloves he was offered. Then they fell on one another like two furious beasts. The bully carried more weight, but the Argonaut dodged him by swift footwork and skilful turns of the head. They fought a long bout, the Argonauts standing round the ring, and cheering as the bully tired himself out with angry, blundering rushes at his opponent. Then, closing in warily Zeus's son landed a powerful hook above the ear, smashing the skull-bone inside. The chieftain sank to his knees like a felled ox. In a few minutes he was dead. The Argonauts cheered, for one more danger was now cleared from the travellers' path.

They feasted that night in the brutal chief's own hall, crowned the winner with bay-leaves, and sang a deep-throated song, specially composed by Orpheus in honour of their champion. When the sun came back from the world's end next morning, they loosened their hawsers and sailed up the Bosphorus, running before a fresh wind. The sea roughened: they lay low in the troughs, while the cold grey crests curled over them. The crew were soaked with spray, and the wind tasted salt on their lips. The sea seemed huge and their boat very small. Yet through it all the steersman, Tiphys, kept a steady hand on the tiller and the ship banged her way bravely through the choppy waves. Slowly the storm died down. At last the *Argo*'s keel cut through quiet water, while on either side

The Voyage of the 'Argo'

creamed a smooth arc of foam. The steersman grinned. "She's got the wishbone in her teeth," he said. He would not leave the helm till they came safely in the lee of Thrace.

Here they had another strange adventure. For here lived King Phineus, who in this life was blind, yet could foresee the future. His was a wretched life, for the gods had sent the Harpies, whose name means Spoilers or Polluters, to torment him. These were loathsome monsters, vultures with sharp claws, and the faces of women, pale and greedy with hunger. Whenever the blind king sat down to eat, they would swoop on him from the clouds, snatching his food in their claws and fouling his table with the stench of their droppings. From this long misery, Phineus had shrivelled to dirty skin and bone; but when he heard the cheeful voices and confident young footsteps of the Argonauts at his door, he knew hope at last. "Young sirs," he said, "if you are the crew of the good ship *Argo,* you alone can save me from my misery. For an oracle tells me I shall be saved when the sons of the north wind come to my hall. Are they of your company?"

The Argonauts pitied the old man, helpless in his degrading hunger and filth. Swiftly they set to work. They set a meal, to tempt the Spoilers, while the two sons of the north wind stood by at the ready, with keen swords drawn. The old king was helped to the table, and swallowed a few feeble mouthfuls when like a whirlwind the Spoilers fell from the clouds with peacock screams. Instantly the two sons of the north wind spread scarlet wings and took off, chasing the Harpies through the sky with the icy blast of their swords. They would have hacked them to pieces if Zeus had not sent a message. For the lovely rainbow stood in the sky and commanded their wintry storm. "It is not lawful to kill the birds which are the hounds of Zeus; but they will visit Phineus no more."

The godlike young men returned with this promise. Gently they bathed frail old Phineus clean of his filth and cooked a savoury dinner, which he ate like a man in a dream. Afterwards they all sat round a cheerful hearth fire in the centre of his hall, and Phineus told them things which he knew by the inward eye of knowledge. He told how Colchis, where they were bound, was rich in horses and sheep, and how the people panned for gold in its river, by trailing sheep's fleece to trap the glittering grains.

He also told them every stage of their journey to its end, warning them of dangers on the way. "But how shall I manage when I get there?" asked Jason anxiously. "Ask me no more questions," said Phineus, "but trust in Aphrodite." Jason was puzzled. What could pleasure-loving Aphrodite have to do with a strenuous voyage of exploration? But the blind seer only smiled his wintry old smile and would say no more.

Next day the heroes rowed away. On Phineus's advice they took a small, grey, wild dove with them. Before them lay their greatest danger, the perilous, mist-shrouded mouth of the Black Sea. As they rowed near to it, even their brave hearts sank. Ahead two mountainous ice-floes, the Clashing Rocks, drifted together, clashed with a noise of thunder and dragged themselves apart again with shuddering groans. All around the sea boiled in clouds of spray mast-high. Between these Clashing Rocks they must steer their boat.

Now they saw that the little soft dove would be their pilot in these cruel waters. As the ice-floes tore themselves apart, Jason launched her, throwing her into the air from his two hands, with a winged prayer. Breathless, they watched her flight. The sea bellowed in its caverns, the spray shot up to darken the sky, but the dove flew bravely on. Swiftly she passed through as the ice clashed together again, and came safely out on the far side. Only her tail feathers were nipped off. The oarsmen cheered her, watching for their chance to follow. "Now, you men!" shouted Tiphys, "Row your hardest! The rocks are parting again!" Like one man they dragged on the oars with all their might. A mountainous wave rose before them and swept them helplessly back, but then another rose behind them sweeping them on. The gods came to their aid, for behind them, unseen, Athena pushed the *Argo* with her mighty arm. As the Clashing Rocks rushed together again, ready to smash her in pieces, the ship shot through the narrowing channel like an arrow. The mascot on their stern, like the dove's tail-feathers, was trapped and broken off, but they were safe through into the Black Sea.

They journeyed on, camping by night and rowing by day, round the shores of the inland sea, meeting tribes and cities as Phineus had foretold. After many days' labour, their journey came to its end on the farthest shore of the Black Sea. The long beach lay, held in the arms of the bay; a river thrust its way through reed beds to the sea. The Argonauts lowered sail and stowed the mast.

On their left hand was the smoke of hearth-fires and the distant barking of dogs. There lay the city and the palace of rich King Aeetes with its fabled courtyards, soaring columns, and fountains running wine and oil, so great was the wealth of his gold-bearing land. On their left was a dark forest. There lay the sacred grove, where the unsleeping snake kept watch and the golden fleece hung on its leafy oak tree. There was nothing near at hand but the cry of birds and the hungry muttering of the sea along the shore. It was a **desolate** place. Here at their journey's end, the Argonauts rested and waited for the dawn.

Jason wins the Golden Fleece

"GENTLE words have great power," said Jason to his friends in the morning. "Let me go first and speak with King Aeetes." Hera sent a kindly mist, in which he crossed the plain and entered the palace courtyard unseen. Aeetes came out to meet a guest, but frowned when he saw a Greek had dared to enter the Black Sea. Jason had never been more handsome or more charming, as he explained courteously how he had been sent to fetch the golden fleece. Aeetes burst into a thunderous rage. "It is not the fleece you want, but my throne," he shouted. "If you were not a guest and therefore sacred, I would tear out your tongue and cut off your hands. Get out of my sight!" But Jason, true to his breeding, said only "Fate has sent me here, not my own will. Be generous and your name will live for ever."

Aeetes gave a contemptuous laugh. "I will give you the fleece when I have tried you. I have two bulls; their bronze hooves tear up the ground and their bronze nostrils snort fire. I yoke them to plough my field of war. Then I sow the furrows with dragon's teeth. Armed men spring up, whom I cut down and harvest like corn, all in one day. Do the same," said Aeetes with a grim smile," and the fleece is yours!" Jason looked at the

Jason wins the Golden Fleece

swarthy, slant-eyed king. "It is my fate," he answered "I must do it if it kills me."

At that moment the king's graceful young daughter, Medea, crossed the courtyard. She was a priestess of Hecate and a witch herself. She should have been at the temple, serving the witch-goddess with offerings of food left at crossroads and the blood of murdered persons, but great Hera had kept her at home on purpose that day. And now Aphrodite, who favours handsome young men, came to Jason's rescue. For Medea saw the stranger and her heart stood still. She forgot honour, duty to her father, the risks she must run. She was on fire for Jason and trembled under the lash of love. Jason went back to the ship with a heavy heart and told his friends what he must do. They heard him without a word, looking at one another in despair.

No one thought of Medea. Yet the young girl had no rest that night. Pacing the room, barefoot and in her nightgown, she remembered Jason's every look and word. At last, tears running down her cheeks, she went and fetched the medicine chest in which she kept her drugs. For Medea had a secret garden in which she grew witches' plants, both healing and deadly: peony to staunch blood, poppy and mandragora to bring sleep, wolf's-bane to kill. She took out an anaesthetic salve, brewed by night from the yellow crocus of the land. "It is a dreadful thing I do and I shall surely be found out," she said through her tears, "but yet I cannot help myself. At dawn I will go to Hecate's temple, and give him the magic medicine against the bulls."

She sent Jason word by a crow, whose flapping and cawing Mopsus could interpret. She put on her loveliest dress and a silver veil to go to the temple. The two of them met, and stood face to face, alone. Medea drew the drug from its hiding place in her belt. "Hear me now, beloved stranger," she said, trembling with love. "When your trial is fixed, on the midnight before, bathe in the river alone. Then put on a black robe, dig a pit and sacrifice to Hecate, pouring out before her a pot of honey. Then go, without looking back. In the morning strip and rub your body with this charm. For one day, while it lasts, no fire nor sword can hurt you. And when you sow the dragon's teeth and the armed men spring up from the earth, throw a stone among them. They will fight for it and kill each other. Then you may take the fleece and go in safety." The tears ran down her cheeks at the thought. "But," she said softly, "remember Medea when you are far away, as I shall remember you." At the sight of the young girl's tears, Jason's heart leapt within him, and he swore a rash vow. "Before Zeus and Hera," he said, "we shall marry and only death shall part us."

Jason sacrificed as Medea had told him and the dread witch-goddess came, garlanded with snakes and with all the hounds of hell barking round her, to accept his offering. The day came. Aeetes dragged out his adamantine plough in the midst of the people, and loosed his fiery bulls from the smoky den where they slept. Jason felt power course through his body. The bulls charged him, breathing flame, but he felt nothing, and parried them easily with his shield.

He took one brazen bull by the horns, and drove it down on its knees with a sharp kick. The other bull charged and he did the same, forcing the pair under the heavy wooden yoke. Then he took the dragon's teeth in a helmet and drove a long, straight furrow, goading the fiery bulls forward with his spear. The bulls bellowed angrily and breathed clouds of flame, but were forced to obey, for their fire did not even make Jason flinch. He ploughed four acres, scattering fistfuls of dragon's teeth behind him as he went. When the field was ploughed and sown, Jason wiped the sweat off his brow with a tanned forearm, filled the helmet with water from the river and drank.

By now the deadly crop was growing, helmets and spears thrusting like blades of winter wheat through the earth. Soon the fighters and their armour shone like stars on a frosty night. Jason was not afraid. He remembered what the young witch had said. He picked up a large stone and hurled it among them. Then the armed men yelled the battle yell, and rushed together with loud clash of armour, fighting and felling one another like pine trees in a gale. Jason had only to draw his sword and hack his way through them to harvest his crop.

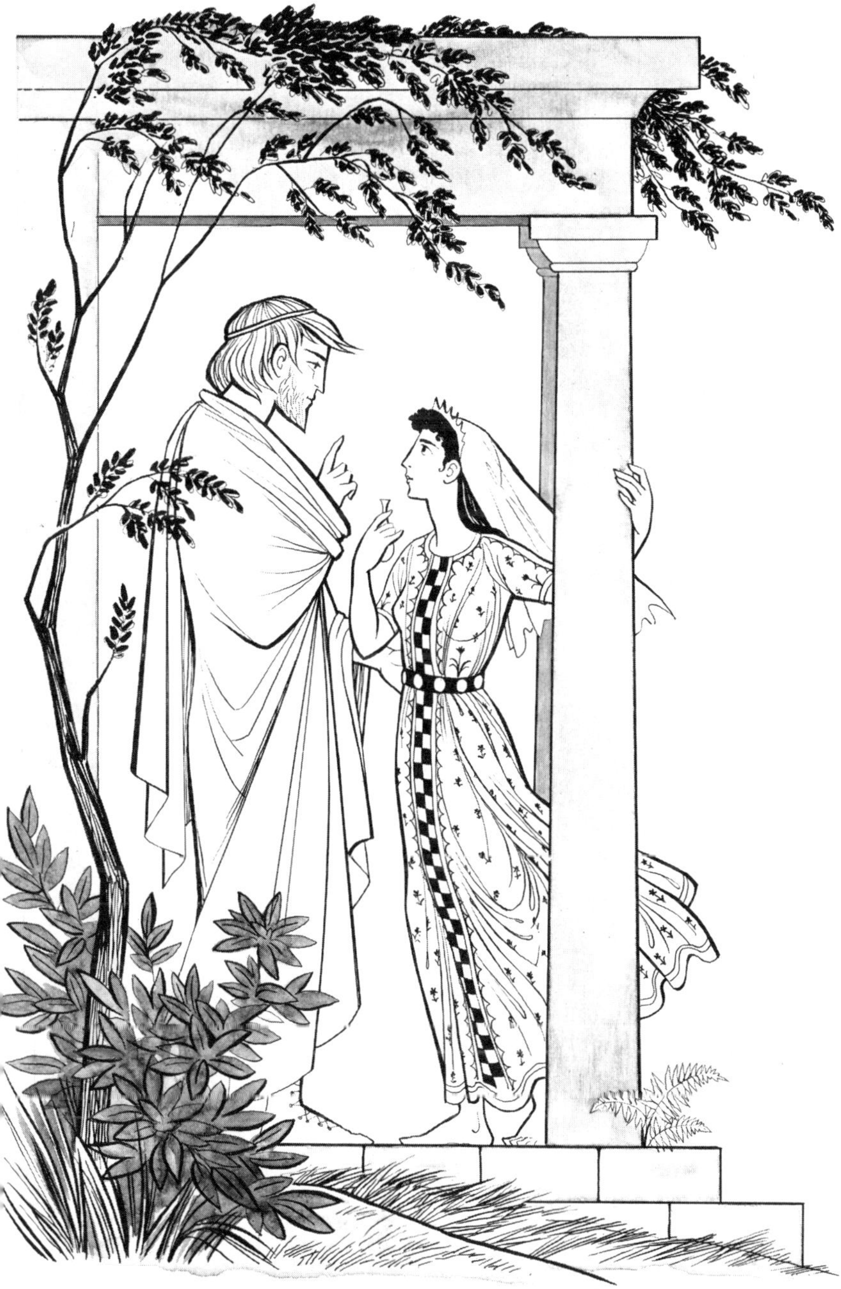

Aeetes howled in rage and amazement. The sun set and Jason's task was done.

But Aeetes would not keep his word. Like a barbarian, he swore he would keep the golden fleece and kill the Argonauts. All that night he plotted murder, while Medea trembled with agonizing fears. She was sure her father would guess what she had done and although she was a witch, yet she was a young girl too. She wept on her pillow, for Aphrodite is a goddess without mercy, bringing sorrow as well as joy.

At last Medea got up. She kissed her bed, she kissed the doorpost and stroked the walls of the room where she had been a child. She cut off a lock of black hair to leave for her mother. "Mother, take this," she said, "for I am going far away where I shall never see you again."

She looked round her room for the last time. "Farewell home, and all it holds," she whispered. Then she ran barefoot through the palace, where locked doors opened themselves at her secret spells. Swiftly and fearfully she ran through the city by narrow back ways, out of the gates and over the empty plain, to where the Argonauts' camp fire crackled beside the ship.

Medea flung herself at Jason's feet and clutched his knees. "Save me and save yourselves, for my father is coming to kill you!" Jason hesitated. He would not show fear before his friends, who meant more to him than any woman. Medea grew frantic. "I will put the snake to sleep; I will give you the golden fleece. Only remember the vow you made to me!" Then Jason understood how Aphrodite would win him the fleece. He vowed aloud before the gods and all the *Argo*'s company, that he would marry Medea and take her home as his wife.

It was earliest morning, still dark. Medea guided the Argonauts as they rowed along the seashore to the sacred wood. They landed near the clearing where the heaven-sent ram had first rested after its flight. Medea took Jason's hand and led him through the wood. There before them was the huge oak tree and on it the fleece, lighting up the spreading branches like golden clouds at dawn. The snake which never slept lay coiled round the trunk: when it saw them it stretched out its head and hissed terribly.

Distant sleepers heard it in their dreams and woke in fear, even the babies. But Medea knew the snake well. As Hecate's priestess she had often brought it honey cakes. Now she sang to it in her sweet young girl's voice, a soft song, a lullaby. The sagacious beast recognized her voice and stirred its coils lazily; snakes love music. It rippled with pleasure through all its length, enchanted by her song. Yet still it watched them. Then Medea, crooning a spell, dipped a sprig of juniper in her most potent drug and sprinkled it over the scaly head. In spite of itself the guardian snake's horny eyelids drooped, and its head sank slowly to the ground. Sleep overwhelmed it in great waves. At last it lay slack and still round the roots of the sacred tree.

Medea called softly and Jason ran though the wood to snatch the golden fleece from its bough. Its shimmering softness enfolded him from shoulder to ankle, casting a golden glow on his face and over the ground where he trod. He was glad, yet mortally afraid in that forbidden holy place. "Come back to the ship," he urged Medea, and together they ran through the sacred grove. So Jason stole both the fleece and the girl, though she was willing. He married Medea in a cave on the homeward voyage, spreading the golden fleece in shining glory to be their marriage bed. Many troubles lay before Jason, for even the most bewitching of witches makes a dangerous wife. He broke faith with Medea at last, and she took a terrible revenge by killing her own children. Jason died in grief-stricken old age, mourning past friendships and glories. Yet where the *Argo* had explored, other Greek ships followed, trading in gold, corn and amber from those perilous shores. The Argonauts were always remembered as a happy company of heroes, and girls spent summer evenings singing of their names and deeds.

Theseus and the Bandits

ATHENS was the greatest of Greek cities, famous in song and story, shining on its high citadel, and crowned at evening with violet light. The piloting of this city lay in the hands of good men, trusted from father to son. Yet in the days of King Aegeus the fate of Athens looked black. For the king had no son, and he feared with good reason that his kinsmen might war for his throne. Then on a journey he visited the king of Troezen. It was a small city, blue with wood smoke, built roughly of stones and pine logs, where a wild ravine plunges to the sea.

There Aegeus married Aethra, the king's young daughter, and lived in love with her, yet did not dare to take her home, for fear his enemies would kill her. When he left he said to her. "Aethra, if you bear a son, bring him up safely in secret here in Troezen, and when he is old enough, send him to me in Athens." "How shall I know when he is old enough?" asked Aethra. For answer Aegeus lifted up a heavy rock called the Altar of Strong Zeus; then he hid his royal sword and a pair of sandals, the ancient symbols of kingship, in the earth beneath. "When he is strong enough to lift this rock," he said, "let him take the sword and shoes and bring them to me in Athens. By

Theseus and the Bandits

these signs I shall know him." For where the earliest heroes, Perseus and Heracles, were sons of Zeus, the heroes of later days had to be strong in their own human wisdom and courage.

Then Aegeus said farewell to Aethra, who watched him go with a heavy heart. He sailed across the sea to his own city, without knowing whether he had begotten a son or not. He sought out oracles. He even married the witch, Medea, Jason's divorced wife, who had murdered her own children, because he hoped she might give him sons by sorcery. Meanwhile Aethra, alone in the headland pastures of Troezen, bore a sturdy son. She called him Theseus, but as Aegeus had warned her, kept his father's name a secret. Theseus was brought up to a rough and simple life.

The king's hall at Troezen stood in its crown of hills, open to the winds and the sky. Blue mountain lupins grew wild around its doors. Theseus rode bare-back in that country of horsemen and learnt to break the wild colts in, with a gentle hand on the reins. He hunted buck or boar with his friends in the woods, and grilled the meat over camp fires they had lit themselves. He learnt to wrestle, fast and skilled of hand, with a mind to match. Above all, his grandfather taught him in that small kingdom that the first duty of a ruler was to deal justly with all men, rich or poor.

"Give your servants all their pay,
  Keep your word without delay."
was the favourite saying of the old king.

Theseus grew to sixteen years old and cut off his hair in front, as a fighting man should, so that no enemy could catch him by it. The hair at the back he left long, for he was determined never to run away from a fight. All this time he was wondering secretly, yet not daring to ask, who his real father was. Now Aethra knew the time had come to tell him. They went out from the king's house, through the rustling pine woods, where the river glinted far below in its shadowy gorge. In a clearing she pointed to the altar, a heavy stone slab meshed in lichen and grass. "Try to lift the stone," she said. At first, angry and ashamed, Theseus could not shift it. Then he gave a great heave and tipped it over, showing earth and torn roots. Dusty gold flashed in the daylight, from sword-hilt and shoe buckles. "Those are your father's sword and shoes which he left here before you were born," said Aethra, not showing her sorrow. "Take them and go to him in Athens, where he is high king. A ship will carry you across the sea in safety." "No," said Theseus. "The sandals tell me I must walk and the sword tells me I must fight for my kingdom. I will go by the land road." All his mother's tears and prayers could not break his will.

Greece is divided in two by a narrow neck of land, in places not more than an hour's walk across. All travellers from north to south had to cross this barrier. The narrow road wound through rocks and pine forests which were a deadly nest of robbers. Theseus hoped, like the hero Heracles, whom he had once seen as a child, to free the land from dangers. He put on a hunter's cap and tunic of fringed leather, buckled on the royal sandals and slid his father's sword through his belt. Then he set out on the stony road through the neck, where dry grasses bend in the salt wind and the blue sea glitters on either side. Dusty cypress trees made thickets by the wayside where the bandits hid. This was the road Theseus chose: it was to lead him through a long life of danger and brave deeds.

He had not gone far before, with a rush of heavy footsteps, a burly man ran out and tried to hit him over the head with a loaded stick. Theseus had not trained as a wrestler for nothing; he calmly side-stepped, caught the bandit's right arm and pressed where the nerve runs near the skin. The club fell to the ground with a clatter. Theseus picked it up and knocked the bully out with one well-placed blow. He slept that night in a pine wood, enjoying the sharp-scented air. Next morning early, he came up to a man who was tugging on a rope, to bring a pine tree down to earth. "Give me a hand with this tree!" he gasped. "Oh no," said Theseus. "I know you! You are the man they call the pine-bender. If I took hold of that tree you would do what you've done to other travellers—let go suddenly, and send me hurtling through the air to be dashed to pieces on the rocks. If you want to steal my wallet, you must fight me for it." The man rushed at him in a rage. Theseus wrestled scientifically and overpowered him. Then he drew down two pine trees till they touched the ground, tied the wretched man between them and let go. The trees sprang back with groaning trunks, but could not drown the screams of the robber they tore apart, while Theseus went coolly on his way.

Now the road wound upward until it became a narrow path leading round a cliff. On one side the rock-face rose sheer to the sky; on the other the sea roared hungrily far below. Theseus rounded a buttress and saw a ledge where a few hardy sea-pinks grew in the crannies and a spring bubbled out of the rock. There sat a red-faced, heavy-shouldered man with one foot in the water. "Who may you be, young stranger?" he shouted. "I am a traveller to Athens," answered Theseus politely. "Then you must pay my toll and wash my feet," said the bully. "If not I will kick you over the cliff." Theseus looked down. The rocks were littered with dead men's bones. "I have heard of you," said Theseus. "You would kick me over anyway."

Young as he was, Theseus knew how to keep a clear head. Stooping swiftly, he dashed water with both hands in the bully's face. Spluttering and bellowing the man gripped him round the waist, but Theseus was lighter, cleverer, fast as a wild mountain cat. He twisted free as they rocked to and fro on the narrow ledge. Then with one heave he threw the bandit out into the empty blue air, watching his body spin in space as it fell to the sea below. A huge splash and a pillar of spray was the end of the robber, though the country people swear he still haunts those cliffs in the shape of a violent north wind which blows travellers to their death. Theseus calmly cooked supper in his black cooking-pot and slept the night in his cave.

Next morning he wound down from the cliff to the cities by the shore. Here at Eleusis was a famous wrestler Cercyon, who challenged all passers-by to a bout. He would seize them round the ribs with powerful arms and slowly squeeze the breath of life out of them. Theseus gracefully accepted Cercyon's challenge and stripped for the match. The women murmured in pity to see his slender young body, so soon to be crushed. But where Cercyon fought with his hands, Theseus fought with his head. He waited till the great ox-like man was tired, then caught him round the knees using Cercyon's own weight to throw him. The big man landed on his head and broke his neck. Ever after men showed the flat space where Theseus threw Cercyon and invented a new science of wrestling.

Now Theseus was near the end of his journey. On the last hill before he came in sight of Athens stood a fortress. Chained watchdogs barked in the still air, and warned by them the owner came out to meet Theseus. "Do me the honour to pass the night in my house," he said, showing yellow teeth in a wolfish smile. "I have good beds for all sorts of travellers; take your choice." Theseus accepted and they entered the dark, charnel-smelling house. "That bed looks rather small," said Theseus, doubtfully. "No matter," said the host pointing to a dog-toothed saw on the wall. "I can trim your legs to fit it." "That one is very long," said Theseus to gain time. He knew he had made a bad mistake and must fight his way out. "No matter," said the bandit again, picking up a massive hammer. "I'll beat you long and thin enough to fill it!" But Theseus thrust out a leg and tripped him up. Then he seized the hammer and belaboured the bandit on his own bed, till the life was hammered out of him.

Theseus had no further adventures on the way. Yet as he walked the last miles he thought deeply. "This is a land without law," he said to himself, "and a road where no traveller is safe. When I am king I will have a straight stone way, level and paved, sounding with the tramp of horses, and on it my people will come and go without fear." Then he broke off, for he saw before him the citadel of Athens, against the darkening sky. The lights of the city sparkled in the pure air like evening stars, and high above them shone his father's hall.

The people came out from their walls to meet him. No one knew who he was, but the story of how he killed the robbers had travelled before him on the road. They led him, bathed and scented, into the king's hall. There sat Aegeus, noble but grey-haired and weary. There beside him sat Medea, slant-

Theseus and the Bandits

eyed, watchful and dangerous. Life had dealt hardly with her; no one would recognize the young girl who fell in love with Jason. Yet she was still a witch. Alone of all the people there, she recognized Theseus for what he was, a threat to her own children.

Medea went swiftly to her chest of drugs, the same she had brought from Colchis. She took a flask of aconite, which peasants call wolf's-bane; a few drops will kill a man. These few drops Medea mixed in a gold cup of wine and carried to the guest, whispering to the old king that she would rid him of an enemy. Theseus courteously lifted the cup to pledge his host, when the torchlight flickered on the sword-hilt in his belt. It was of ivory and gold, carved with the house-snake of Athens, a weapon for a king. Theseus was in the act of putting the cup to his lips, when suddenly—"Where did you get that sword?" cried Aegeus sharply. "Sir, I found it under a stone," answered Theseus, the gold beaker held between them. "You are my son!" cried the old king, dashing the poisoned cup from his hands. It fell to the floor with a clash and rolled over the stones, trickling dark dregs. Medea howled, a wild and savage cry, as her father had howled long ago, when Jason escaped his vengeance. She rushed from the hall, leapt into her witch's flying chariot, whipped up her pair of flying dragons, and was never seen again in Athens.

But Aegeus kissed Theseus, called all the people of Athens together, and proclaimed him true heir. The scheming kins men broke into revolt, but Theseus fought and scattered them all. Then the people lit fires on every altar in the city and led garlanded beasts to the sacrifice in thanksgiving. Nobles and working men feasted together in the streets to welcome the new prince. "Bravest of heroes," they shouted, clashing their cups together, "your people drink a health to you!" There was never more joy in Athens than at the coming of Theseus, the king's true son.

Theseus slays the Minotaur

Feasts are soon over, and the sound of flutes vanishes on the air. A prince must share his people's dangers and bear their troubles on his own back. Minos, the king of Crete, had a quarrel with Athens because his son had been killed at the Athenian games. Crete was a rich and powerful kingdom, a land of gold, where Athens was a land of stone. So Minos made war on Aegeus, defeated him and forced him to pay tribute every year. This tribute was not of money, but of lives. Each spring seven young men and seven girls were sent across the seas to Crete. There they vanished into the vast, labyrinthine palace of Minos at Cnossos, and not one had ever returned.

April came, in the year of Theseus's coming, and the tribute was due for the third time. Silent families gathered in the market place below the citadel, to draw lots as the custom of Athens was. Theseus saw the grief of the parents whose children's names were called. Their mothers brought them food in a basket for the journey, and told them tales of the heroes Perseus and Heracles to hearten them, even through their tears. Theseus's heart burned within him at the sight. "Father," he said, "it is a shameful thing to send these children to die. Send me with them and I will do my best to save them."

Theseus slays the Minotaur

Aegeus was old, the strength-giving sun could no longer warm him. Now he looked like a man sick to death. "You are all the sons I have, Theseus, and you must be king of Athens," he said. "How can men follow," argued Theseus, "if the king does not lead?" So Aegeus consented with grief. He gave his son a white ship's sail.

"If you return," he said, "hoist this white sail, that I may see it far away on the water and know you are safe. If I see a black sail, I shall know that the gods have taken my son from me." They clasped hands and parted.

The ship with a black sail crossed the sea from Athens to the island of Crete. Gulls circled round the mast, dolphins rolled and tumbled in the waves alongside, but few stood on the prow to watch their sport, or enjoy the sun glinting on dark blue water. The seven young men and seven girls aboard knew they were going to their death. Some believed the old wives' tale that they would be eaten alive by the Minotaur, a monster half-man, half-bull, which lived in a dark labyrinth under the palace at Cnossos. Others had heard travellers' tales of perilous games on a polished dancing floor, where prisoners were sent out naked and unarmed to meet wild bulls. Not one hoped to return. Theseus stood apart from the rest, his strong fists clenched on the gunwale, his face turned towards the sea. An oracle had told him to ask Aphrodite's help, and it was to this lovely, wayward goddess he prayed. "O lady, whose spells rest on the eyelids of boys and girls, it is for young lives I plead. I have sworn to face the monster in the dark labyrinth and free us from this tribute of beloved children for ever. I have willed it so, and my courage will not fail. Only help me, Aphrodite of the sudden glances." But the sea and the sky gave no answer and the black ship continued her journey to Crete.

The palace of Minos at Cnossos was old while Athens was still young: a vast courtyard surrounded by buildings complex as a city. Outside were porches, where squat black columns framed a view of thirsty hills. Within lay a maze of halls, dark passages and deep stair-wells, where no stranger could find his way. Even bold Theseus felt a chill in his heart as they were herded into the throne-room of Minos. The walls were close covered with paintings. They showed jewelled, wasp-waisted men, priestesses with flashing eyes who clenched writhing serpents in their hands, acrobats leaping the backs of long-horned bulls or dying under their feet.

In royal Crete the bull was god, for Zeus in bull disguise had founded their house. Now his descendant, Minos, sat high on a throne to count his living tribute. Beside him sat a young girl dressed in the Cretan fashion, with bare, painted breasts, flounced skirts and crown of gold leaves. The princess Ariadne led a haunted life. The only pleasure she knew was to watch the contests in the bull ring, when young men and women, naked like wrestlers, seized the bull by its deadly horns and vaulted over its back. Often at night her sleep was broken by bellowing or wild cries from the prison labyrinth below the palace. Now she looked at the young captive prince from Athens, his thoughtful eyes and wrestler's stance. She knew he would meet his death sooner or later at the bull's sharp horns. "It is well," said Minos with a smile of cruel pleasure. "Take them away."

Theseus and his companions were driven into the labyrinth to wait for their call. The gates were opened and clanged shut behind them. Ariadne watched the captives from Athens as they were driven out day by day into the bull ring, to dance their weaving circle round the maddened beasts. She trembled inwardly to see Theseus, stripped and oiled, run in to take the bull by the horns and vault soaring over its back. The gods stiffened his spirit, giving him skill of hand and force of mind; he was quick as a dolphin in the sea. Ariadne questioned and learned how the prince had not been chosen by lot, but had come of his own free will to share danger with his friends. She saw young men and girls broken and bleeding on the patterned stones and was suddenly weary of her life in the black, blood-drenched palace. Aphrodite, light of foot and light of heart, never had easier work to do than in this young girl's spirit.

Ariadne had a secret. The master craftsman who built the many-chambered labyrinth had given her a magic ball of thread, which would roll along, unwinding as it went, and guide one to the innermost depths where the Minotaur lived.

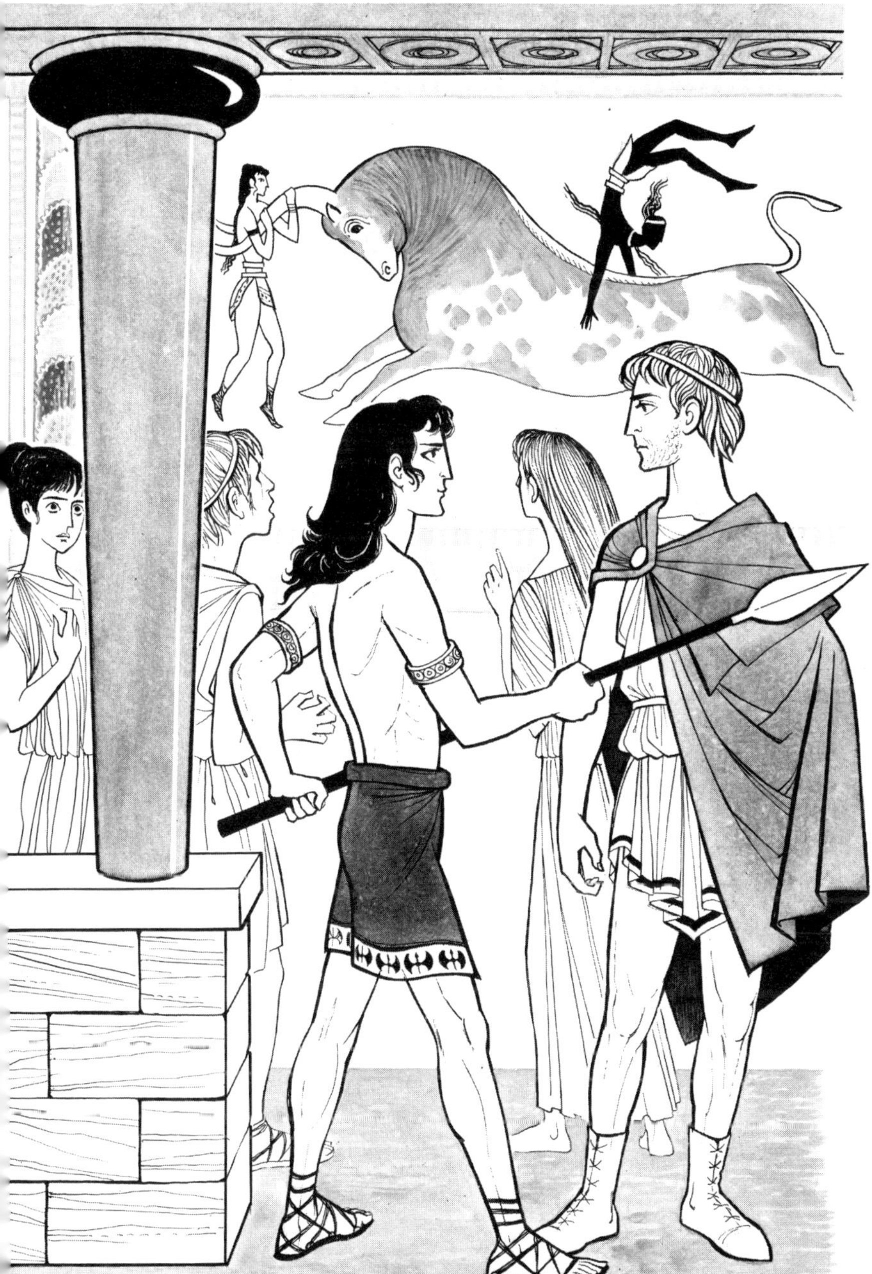

One night she gave the guards drugged wine and unlocked the doors of the prison with oiled keys, silently. In the darkness beside him, Theseus heard a whisper. "I am Ariadne, daughter of Minos. I will help you to kill the Minotaur, if you will swear to take me back to Athens as your wife." Now Theseus knew that Aphrodite had answered his prayer. Gladly he promised, and the princess led him softly to an iron gate. She unlocked it and put a ball of thread into his hand. "Hold this thread, and it will unwind to guide you as you go," she said. "I will stay here, holding the other end, to guide you on your journey back. Hold fast; do not drop it, or you will never leave the labyrinth again."

Holding the thread in his hand, Theseus groped his way through the smooth stone corridors of the labyrinth. Walls were all around him, cold, clammy walls, curving and twisting, this way and that, each like the other. Now he came to a blank end, now to a place with many turnings; but the thread unrolled itself smoothly on his cupped palm and he went steadily onwards. The passage narrowed, and when he put up his hand Theseus could feel the slimy stonework overhead. He had reached a crossing place and stood waiting for the thread to lead him, when he heard heavy breathing in the darkness, and footsteps coming slowly towards him. With all the strength of his will, Theseus steadied himself and waited, poised to take a wrestler's hold, while the shuffling steps drew near. There was a silence. Each knew that the other was there, waiting in the dark for the meeting the Fates had willed.

No one has ever known what followed in that dark, underground place. The memory of it was so terrible that Theseus never spoke of it again. Some tellers of tales relate that he killed a monster, half-man, half-bull, with a double-headed axe. Some, more learned, claim that in the labyrinth lived a priest wearing a ritual bull's head mask of gold and waiting in the dark with a sharp knife, to kill the lost, stumbling, terrified victim appointed for the sacrifice. They wrestled there below the ground. A terrible cry echoed through the caverns and galleries of the labyrinth, then all was silent as before. Theseus groped his way with the help of the thread back to the gate

Theseus slays the Minotaur

where Ariadne waited. There was no need for words. She took him by the hand, stole through the sleeping palace, and led him down the chariot-way to the port. There the other young Athenians waited. They had killed their guards, girls fighting as bravely as men for their freedom, and released themselves with stolen keys. They fell upon Theseus with tears, for they had never expected to see him again. They climbed into the black ship, hoisted sail and slipped silently out between the galleys of King Minos at anchor in the bay.

Soon after, the great palace of Cnossos was destroyed by earthquake or fire, to lie for thousands of years in heaped-up ruins. Ruin came too, to the love of Ariadne. For some reason which he never told, Theseus deserted her on the homeward journey, while she lay sleeping on the island of Naxos. Her tears were dried only when the god of the island, Dionysus, took her for his bride. All this time, Theseus crossed the sea towards Athens, setting his course by the friendly stars.

King Theseus

On their journey, the young Greeks put in at Delos, the island where Apollo was born. There a crystal air glitters on rock and sea, and an avenue of stone lions, wind-worn and noble, leads to the sanctuary. It seemed a place of holy light, after the blackness of the labyrinth. They gave thanks to the god, and gravely danced before his altar, the dance of the crane birds in spring. This was the first time in all history that girls and men danced together, united in pure friendship at being still alive. From Delos they had a hard voyage home and food ran low. Theseus put his crew on short rations and all lived gladly, share and share alike. No one cared in that happy company who had been rich at home, or who poor. They wove between the hundred islands towards the great temple of Poseidon on the cape south of Athens. And either from care for his young crew, or from happiness, or because it was written in his fate, Theseus forgot to hoist the white sail.

Every day old King Aegeus went to a rock by the great gate of the citadel, where the temple of Wingless Victory now stands. There he watched while the shadows shrank and the hot hours wore on, day after day. But he saw no beacon-fire on the cape, no horseman or runner on the land, no sail far out at sea. October came with cold nights and the first frosty mornings. Theseus had been seven months away. And at last one day Aegeus saw a sail. The sun shone on it at first, gilding its colour, but as it drew nearer he saw it was black. Then the old king felt such bitter grief at heart that he had sent his son into danger, that he fainted and fell to his death on the rocks below. Ever afterwards the sea he watched has been called by his name, the Aegean.

Theseus landed at the port and sent a runner ahead to tell his father he was safe, but the messenger returned with the news that the old king was dead. Meanwhile the parents of the tribute boys and girls came pouring out of the walls to meet their children, hardly able to believe they had come back from the dead, laughing and crying at once. It was a time for joy, and a time for tears. The people lamented for Aegeus but welcomed Theseus gladly. It was like the winter ritual when the old year dies and the hopeful young new year is born. As a thanksgiving, Theseus put all the ship's stores, now only dried beans, into one huge earthenware pot, in which they cooked and ate together. Ever since, when that day comes round, the Athenians go down to the shore and share a beanfeast, remembering that happy return.

Now Theseus was king indeed. He was young, but the wise gods had let him know suffering, and he who suffers gains strength in his mind. No common ills could break him or drive him back. He saw Greece, a small country, ridged with mountains, torn with clefts, threatened by pirate islands and the wild horsemen and women from the north. He saw a score of city-kingdoms, each on its fortress hill with its own king and army, each tearing its neighbours to death in senseless wars. And Theseus saw beyond the vision of commonplace men: how these cities could agree to share good government and live in peace, learning skilled crafts, storing the harvest against the bad year, rich in grain and grape, richer in men and women. In that kingdom, the sheep-watcher or the fisherman and their wives could be as sure of justice as the richest merchant. Even the little boys who scared birds in the fields would know themselves safe. So Theseus undertook another journey. He went from village to village, from family to family, asking them to join in one Greek commonwealth.

The little towns were proud and jealous. The tale is told of one village of mud huts, where they showed Theseus, nonetheless, a gold cup in every house. Theseus soon saw it was the same gold cup, the only one they possessed, smuggled from house to house by back ways, to impress him. He saw the rulers of cities would always be jealous of his power. So he promised he would no longer be king in Athens, but only a judge. For the rest, he said, "Every citizen, in all and for all, shall have an equal voice." And he found labouring men everywhere glad to trust him. Theseus remembered the teaching of his grandfather: "Keep your word without delay." He gave up his throne as he had promised, the first king ever to do so. He built a Council Chamber and a Law Court in Athens, both of which you may see to this day. There he gave justice, even to household slaves and the foreign women captured in battle, who belonged by custom to their conquerors. He struck a common coinage, stamped with a bull, perhaps remembering his own days in the bull-ring. Everyone was proud to live in Athens, a city of free men. Foreign immigrants came willingly to work there, and Theseus welcomed them as fellow-citizens. They had a right to speak up and be heard in the general meeting when heralds went out through Greece, shouting in every market-place, "All people come ye hither." They came, and spoke their minds.

So Theseus brought his city honour among men. He kept just measure in his thoughts and doings, he was loved for his kindness to strangers and his laws lasted for many generations. From labours in youth should come a calm old age, but for Theseus this was not so. His several marriages all ended badly and he quarrelled with his only son who died before they could be reconciled. The truth was that, like many clever men, he was not wise in his own family; moreover, his very cleverness made enemies. He was often away beyond the frontiers, fighting the Amazons or the wild centaurs. While he was gone a rival politician seized power in Athens, telling the rich Theseus had robbed them by his commonwealth, and the poor, who loved him, that he was dead. "He shut you within the walls of the city," said this supple-tongued man, "only to bend you to his will. Are you any more free now with one lord than you were with many? The freedom Theseus offers you is nothing but a dream." This man and his party defeated Theseus. He may even have sent a secret agent to assassinate him, for Theseus died while he was still abroad, in a mysterious fall from a cliff on the island of Scyros.

The name of King Theseus was not spoken in Athens again and his memory was almost forgotten for several generations. Then Athens had to fight a desperate war against the great empire of Persia in the East. In the roar and dust of battle, many men declared they could feel the spirit of Theseus fighting beside them, fully armed and a mighty wrestler, as in the days when he was king. They told this dream to the priestess of Apollo at Delphi, who said it was a message to bring the bones of Theseus home to Athens and give them honourable burial.

The people of Scyros were a savage race of pirates, but the Athenians sent ships against them, captured the island and began to search for the hasty, unmarked grave of Theseus. One day on a cliff-top they saw a she-eagle, the bird of Zeus, tearing up the stony ground with her talons. The soldiers ran to the spot and dug, sweating under the hot sun, till they struck a stone slab. Beneath it lay a tall skeleton, armed with bronze spear and shield. Reverently, with hymns and prayers, they rowed it back across the Mediterranean Sea to Athens, where they buried it in the enclosure still called the Sanctuary of Theseus. There, ill-treated slaves, over-driven labourers or captive women could take refuge from their tyrants. The refugees prayed and burnt offerings in honour of Theseus, although he was a mortal, not a god. Old men remembered how he had been their grandfathers' protector and how courteously he had listened to the tale of their troubles when they came to him for help. It was as if King Theseus had been alive and had come to live in their city again.

Love and Magic

Three Golden Apples

A GREEK lord in Calydon longed to have a son. When his wife was with child he planned how the young prince would ride beside him at war or hunting, or sit beside him at judgement in his high hall. The day came, his wife was delivered of a child and he rushed to the women's quarters for a first sight of his son. The midwife-slave held out to him the naked, howling body of a new-born girl. Then rage and cruel disappointment possessed the king. "Take the brat away," he shouted. "Leave it on the hillside and never let me see it again!" This was the custom with all unwanted children in Greece. The women wailed, as women will, but any man knew better than to take notice of them. A slave took the child, whom her mother with many tears had named Atalanta, carried her up the steep path and left her to starve among the wild blue lupins. Such deaths were not murder and the king was easy in his mind. He had rid himself of an unwanted girl, with no fear of the Furies pursuing him.

Atalanta would have died of cold and hunger, like thousands of others, but that Artemis, the Lady of the Beasts, passed by and saw her. Though she loved to hunt with her silver bow, her ten brindled hounds and her train of young girls, yet Artemis loved the beasts she hunted. The stag bowed its lofty antlers to her and the brown bear of the forest was her sacred animal. She took the young of beasts and men under her protection, and to honour her little girls danced wearing the pelts of bears.

Artemis pitied Atalanta, the new-born creature wailing its life away upon the mountain side. Autumn was coming with the first frosts. Swiftly the goddess commanded a mother bear to nose the baby into a winter den with her own two cubs. Atalanta lived out her first winter as a little bear. Blind as a cub, she burrowed in the dry leaves of the warm den, or clung to her foster-mother's rich fur. And the bear warmed the little naked creature, suckled her, licked her clean or cuffed her with soft paws, like one of her own brood. Winter ended, the cubs blundered out into the pale spring sunshine and Atalanta, shaggy-headed and blinking, crawled after them, more than half an animal, but alive and strong.

There she was found by a clan of nomad hunters from the north, who carried her back and brought her up in their black tents, eating meat grilled at the camp fire and drinking mare's milk. Atalanta grew up unlike other girls. She did not like to walk to and fro at the loom, or tend the hearth fire or sit telling tales among the spinners. Though beautiful, she would not wear a long robe or crimp her hair in tight plaits. She would rather hunt wild beasts in the shadowy hills, or guard the flocks, leaving her bed in the morning before the stars had set. She grew up like the goddess who protected her, as a hunter. She loved the loud chase over windy headlands, the belling of hounds and the slaying of stags; the woods rang with her hunting call. She swam without fear; the deep lake held her by the waist, where no man dared to lay his arm. She could shoot straight and run faster than any man. Atalanta pitied married housewives, shut up indoors all day, with weary chores and fractious children. A priestess warned her, "Do not take a husband, for if you do, though still living you will lose yourself." Atalanta never fell in love and never wished to marry. She was vowed to Artemis.

Atalanta soon became famous. The king of Calydon, her

Three Golden Apples

father's lord, offended Artemis, so as punishment the goddess sent a savage boar with sharp tusks and angry red eyes to terrorize his land. His son, Prince Meleager, sent heralds to all the cities of Greece, inviting the bravest heroes to come and hunt the boar with him. Atalanta accepted this challenge. Some of the older men refused to hunt in company with a woman, but Meleager insisted. At first sight of Atalanta, unlike all ordinary women, with her bow on her shoulder, her hair tied in a horse's tail, her long brown legs and slender waist, he had fallen deeply in love. Together they hunted the murderous boar through a sedgy hollow. It charged furiously, scattering the hunters and killing two of them, until a swift arrow from Atalanta's bow drew first blood and checked its rush. Meleager killed the boar and gave it to Atalanta in honour of her courage. The older men grew jealous at once. "Leave it alone, woman, and don't interfere with man's work!" they shouted angrily. There was a sudden furious quarrel and a fight in which Meleager killed his own mother's brother.

The Furies compelled the queen to avenge her blood-brother's death. She remembered how, long ago, when her child, Meleager, was born the three Fates spun his destiny. A fire had burnt in the birth-room, and the Fates pointed to a burning log. "The child will live till that log is burned to ashes," they said. At once the mother snatched it from the hearth, flung cold water on it and hid it safely. Now, pale and weeping, she brought the log out and lit kindling wood; she loved her son, but her brother's ghost cried out to her for revenge. As his mother hurled the log on the flames, Meleager felt a burning pain. As the fire blazed up, so did his agony; as it died down, so did his life. All this Atalanta saw, and she wept; she knew the prince had died because he loved her. She remembered the warning of the priestess and longed to live among the beasts in the shady woodland, far from the sight of men.

Because she was now beautiful and famous, Atalanta's father begged her to come home. But his words of greeting were, "Dear child, you must choose a husband and give me a grandson." Atalanta feared, but Artemis, unseen, told her how to escape. "Father I consent," said the girl, "but no man may have me unless he can beat me in a foot race. Let those who try and fail be put to death!" Atalanta believed no one would try, for she was famous as the swiftest runner living, yet to her grief one after another tried and died. Crowds came from far away to watch the races. The quiet valley became a city of tents and camp fires. Among the watchers came a young man of Arcadia, Milanion. "What fool would risk death just to get a wife?" he said laughing as the race began. **Then he saw Atalanta flash past, black hair flying behind her, light tunic blown against her body, sandal ribbons streaming in the wind of her flight.** She was lovely to see in that leaf-garlanded race, and her mind did not dishonour her beauty. She won; the man she had defeated groaned and died, and Milanion, as though in a dream, stepped forward to take his place. "Race against me!" he said.

Atalanta looked at the stranger, so handsome and so young, and for the first time was not sure whether she would rather win or lose. "Do not risk your life for me," she begged, not knowing these were words of love. Her cruel father and the spectators, hungry for a spectacle, clamoured to see the race. Milanion prayed to Aphrodite, "Oh lady, you have lit your flame of love in my heart. Help it to burn brightly." Aphrodite pitied the handsome young mortal. Besides, she was angry with Atalanta for refusing to fall in love. Unseen, the goddess of love glided through the air, bringing a golden bough on which glittered three apples of gold. She gave these to Milanion who hid them in his tunic, while Aphrodite whispered laughing in his ear, to tell him how to win the race.

The trumpets sounded. Both runners sprang forward from the starting-line. They flew over the track like seabirds skimming the waves, while the onlookers shouted themselves hoarse. Atalanta slowed her steps, but was still forced to leave the other runner behind. Milanion gasped and stumbled, his heart pounding, as she drew ahead. Then he drew out one of the golden apples and skilfully bowled it across her path. Atalanta checked at the sight, like a pointer hound. Drawn by the spell of the magic fruit, she ran off her course, stooped and picked it up. Milanion passed her and the crowd roared applause. Then Atalanta spun round and set off, swifter than hare or eagle. Soon she had left her lover far behind again. Once more he threw the lovely fruit, and once more she ran out of her way to pick it up. She could not help herself, for the apples came from the tree of life, whose magic pulls at the heart with desire. Yet still she ran on, fleet as a deer, or a salmon leaping the waterfall. Milanion felt death at his heels. "Help me, oh goddess," he prayed, and hurled the last gleaming apple far off the course. Atalanta tried to resist, but she could not escape what Aphrodite had willed. Driven by love, she rushed upon her fate. As she stooped to gather the apple, Milanion passed the winning post. The crowd cheered, Milanion took her hand and as in a dream swift Atalanta, that wild girl, felt herself led away.

So Aphrodite of the sudden glances conquered chaste Artemis and the wedding was held. Afterwards Milanion led his bride joyfully home to his house in the hills. On the journey, night came, and they sheltered in a cave in the woods, which was a sanctuary of Earth, the mother of gods and men. The two young people cared nothing for this holy place. All they wanted was to be with each other. They talked and laughed in the darkness, whispered and made love, at home in each other's delight as though they had been under their own roof. Fate never forgives those who scorn the gods. She was angry and changed the two lovers into spotted lynxes. So the prophecy came true: Atalanta took a husband and lost herself; yet it was no grief, for they roamed the woods together and the wild forest she loved was their home.

The Hunter and the Nymph

CEPHALUS was a hunter, feared by the wild creatures of the forest, but his wife, the nymph Procris, was loved by beasts and men. The peasants in the villages would leave a bowl of milk outside their doors at night, so that she might visit them and guard their flocks. She was the unseen spirit who brushed away tormenting flies from the muzzle of the ox at the plough. She turned away the straying lamb from the snake coiled among the stones. She knew the call of every bird and could answer them in their own wordless language. She lived beside a spring, where vines still hang down in a curtain of green and water drips cold from the mossy rock. In that glaring, thirsty land her spring seemed holy and all the beasts of the countryside came to drink under her protection.

Cephalus and Procris loved each other. She would not have changed him for a god, and he swore he cared for no other woman, no, not if Aphrodite herself let slip the robe from her polished shoulders. Men called these forest lovers happy, and so they seemed. But call no man happy while he lives; for the gods willed it otherwise.

Procris used to search the hills and ferny dells for the herbs which will heal a wound or calm a fever. These she dried in

The Hunter and the Nymph

bunches which hung from her green trellis roof, and gods and mortals alike came to her for healing. When Zeus was tormented by a headache he called for Procris, whose cool, firm hands soon stroked away his pain. In gratitude he gave her magic **gifts,** which she brought home to Cephalus. "I bring you gifts from Zeus," she said, desiring to share her greatest treasures. A slender long-limbed hound leapt from her side. This was Tempest, Zeus's own hunting dog, so fast it could outrun any creature living. Now it crouched down and laid its brindled head on the foot of its new master. Next Procris gave Cephalus a spear of polished ash wood, tipped with gold. This was the hunting spear of Zeus which never missed its mark, but killed instantly and returned blood-stained to the thrower's hand. Cephalus took these gifts with a hunter's savage joy. He did not know that they would bring him everlasting sorrow.

From that day he was the greatest of hunters. Wolves, mountain bears, wild boars and swift-running deer all fell to his magic spear and hound. Every morning while it was still dark he set out with Tempest at heel to set nets in the forest. There it was that Eos the Dawn first saw him, as she drove the shining chariot of the morning star above the shadowy mountain tops. She was sister to the sun and moon, like them a child of the old Titans, and wild as the sea. She saw the young man, stripped for the hunt, lean and bronzed, and desired to possess him utterly, for herself alone. But Cephalus only shook his head at her honeyed speeches.

"You are queen of the borderland of light and darkness," he said "yet it is Procris I love." "Go back to Procris then," said the goddess through set teeth, "but you will wish you had never had her." Cephalus thought no more of it, forgetting the fate of mortals who scorn the gods. Nor did he see into the heart of rosy-fingered Dawn as she whipped up her sky horses and drove away to brood upon revenge.

Eos began to follow Cephalus upon his hunting expeditions, veiling her brightness behind a cloak of cloud or hiding in the dark woods. He took no huntsmen or horses. The magic spear and hound were all he needed. He left when the sun's first ray netted the hill-top and coursed till he was breathless and sweating in the full heat of noonday. One day when he had tracked a stag for hours through the forest, he came to a cool glade. He threw off his deerskin cloak, unbuckled the belt with his bronze skinning-knife, and flung himself down to rest. Cool shadows closed round him, a woodpecker drummed in the trees and a soft breeze ruffled his hair. Fate, which no man can escape, led him to speak to the light-winged wind. "It is because of you I love the woods and wild places so much; your breath on my lips brings coolness and pleasure." Eos, who had been listening unseen, stole away through the trees. "Now I shall have my revenge," she whispered. "I shall tell Procris that Cephalus is making love to the forest nymphs; when jealousy stabs her heart she will suffer as I have suffered!"

Aphrodite is a goddess not to be denied and those under her spell are no longer masters of themselves. She gives pain, as well as pleasure to gods and men in love. So now she made the lovely Dawn ugly with jealousy. Eos hurried to Procris and whispered in her ear. "Cephalus, whom you believe yours, sings love songs to the nymphs in the forest. Come with me and hear for yourself how he praises their beauty." Love makes us ready to believe fearful things. Procris fainted away with shock and grief. After a long time she came to herself, in doubt and misery. There is no pain more cruel than love. Her rival was the empty air, but she suffered as though it were a real woman. Yet still she was loyal in love. "I will not believe it," she said, "unless I see it with my own eyes."

Next day Cephalus left home as usual at dawn and went to the woods, but this time Eos led Procris after him. "Creep in there where the trees are thickest," said Eos. "There you can see and hear without being seen." Procris longed to refuse, but doubt and dread, stronger than herself, drove her into the thicket. Her green tunic vanished among the tangled branches and not the trembling of a leaf gave warning she was there. She saw Cephalus, her lover, tired from hunting, lie on the grass with heavy-limbed grace, and bare his body to the summer wind. "Come to me," he murmured to the summer wind; "come to me now, my pleasure, my beloved friend."

It was true, thought Procris, that he loved a forest nymph,

and she sighed, a sigh too soft for human ears to catch. But the brindled hound heard it and pricked up its ears, for it knew the voice of its gentle mistress. With a joyous bark the dog plunged into the thicket. Cephalus, too, was on his feet in an instant, tiredness forgotten. He had the hunter's instinct to defend himself from lurking dangers. Perhaps the hound had scented a lynx or a wild boar in the undergrowth. Cephalus poised his spear, the spear which could never miss its mark, and hurled it with all his strength into the thicket. He heard the branches snap, as if something had fallen to the ground. "Cephalus, alas Cephalus," cried a soft voice, and he recognized Procris. "Where are you?" he cried in sudden fear. No wild beast had ever chilled him with such dread. "Here in the thicket," she answered. "I am dying."

Cephalus burst in among the trees, tearing his way through the undergrowth in terror like one of the beasts he had so often killed. Procris was lying where she had fallen, weakly struggling to pull the magic spear she had given him from her own breast. He lifted her up, carried her to the glade and laid her on a soft bed of pine-needles. He tried to bind her wound with linen torn from his own tunic, but her strength was ebbing with her blood. Yet she still tried to speak. "By the love we have shared, do not take the nymph of the forest in my place."

Then Cephalus understood her grief and told her the truth. She could not answer but seemed at peace. So long as she could see she gazed up at the open sky, where the sun still took his godlike way to the west. Then she closed her eyes and died. Her spring among the rocks ceased its murmur, dwindled to a trickle and died away for ever, for its guardian nymph had gone. Lacking its cool drops the flowers of the forest began to fade. The creatures of field and forest, whom Procris had loved, knew that death had taken their protector from them. As for Cephalus, he still hunted and men envied him the magic spear which could not miss its mark. Yet often his eyes filled with tears when he remembered what the gods had willed it should cost him. So ended the love of Cephalus and Procris.

The Tasks of Psyche

"Once upon a time there lived a king and queen who had three daughters." These comfortable words begin a fairy story told by grandmothers on sunlit doorsteps all over the ancient world. "The two elder daughters were handsome, but the youngest, named Psyche, was the loveliest girl ever seen. Her sisters married but she stayed at home, and people came from far countries just to look at her, as though she were a statue. They swore she must be Aphrodite come to earth again, and strewed garlands round her pretty feet as she passed by. Meanwhile the real Aphrodite saw her temples deserted, her statues uncrowned and her altars unswept. Jealous and angry she summoned her winged son, called by the name of Cupid, and pointed out Psyche. 'Pray you dear child,' she said, 'avenge your mother. Make that silly mortal girl fall in love with the most poor, crooked, vile, miserable creature living.' Cupid took his bow and arrows of desire and flew off to obey her—or so she thought.

Time passed and no one dared to marry Psyche, who seemed like a young goddess, too high for mortal love. The poor girl moped till her father went to ask an oracle to find her a husband. Perhaps Aphrodite prompted the answer, which

The Tasks of Psyche

was this. 'Dress Psyche like a corpse and set her on a high hill. There a deadly dragon will fly by and seize her for his wife.' The people all wept as they carried Psyche with black torches and funeral hymns to a high rock where they left her alone, wiping her tears with her wedding weil. Then the south wind blew, strong yet soft. It floated Psyche down from the hill to a deep valley and laid her on a grassy bank, where, tired out from fear and crying she fell asleep. She woke and wandered through this strange land, following a river which led her into a shady wood.

In the heart of the wood she came to an enchanted castle, with pillars and pavements of gold. The porches glittered like sunshine, lighting up the trees. There was not a lock or bolt on the doors and not a soul to be seen. 'All that you see is yours to command,' said a voice. Dreamily, Psyche walked in through the shining doors. Unseen hands laid a table and served delicious food. Unseen harps and sweet voices made music as she ate. The hands filled a scented **bath,** dressed her in a delicate nightgown and laid her in bed. In the night Psyche woke to find an unseen husband by her side. 'My sweet wife,' he said, holding her in his arms, 'one thing I pray you. Never try to see me, or great sorrow will come to us both.' 'Oh my sweetheart, my joy,' she cried, 'whoever you may be, even though I may never see your face, I would rather die than part from you!' For there are secret keys which unlock the doors of love, and already Psyche loved her husband. Then she fell asleep and in the morning found herself alone.

Days passed and all day, though the hands waited on her, Psyche was alone. One night her husband found her in tears of loneliness, and promised her sisters might come to visit her. The wind caught them up and wafted them softly to her door. When they came into the fairy palace, there was kissing and greeting. The music played, they ate sweet things from golden dishes, Psyche showed them her lovely house and filled their laps with jewels before they left. 'My husband is bald as a coot,' said one sister as they went home. 'Mine has gout and keeps me short of money,' said the other bitterly, 'but that goose Psyche is married to some lord who gives her all his treasure.'

So, in an evil hour, envy crept into their hearts and they began to plot against her. They visited the enchanted palace again and again, prying into everything and plaguing Psyche with questions. 'Who is your husband?' they demanded. Psyche was a scatter-brained creature. First she said her husband was a young man, always out hunting. Next time, forgetting, she said he was a rich merchant with a grey beard. 'She is lying. She has never seen him,' thought the sisters. 'Perhaps she is married to some god!' Envy devoured them at the thought. At last Psyche admitted she had never seen her husband. 'A dire, fierce serpent full of deadly poison lies by your side each night,' said the sisters promptly. 'Take this sharp razor and a burning lamp. When he is asleep, cut his head off; then we will marry you to some handsome lord.' They went off, pleased with their day's work, leaving poor foolish Psyche in tears.

That night she could bear her curiosity no longer. When her husband fell asleep, she fetched razor and lamp from the niche where she had hidden them and crept barefoot back, dreading to see the deadly dragon in her bed. There lay a glorious, godlike man asleep. His bright hair covered the pillow; beside him lay a golden bow and arrows and soft rustling plumage of two great wings rested quietly at his back. Cupid had defied his mother and secretly married Psyche himself. Such beauty makes the heart-strings tremble like a harp. Psyche embraced and kissed her husband with joy, but as she stooped to wind her arms around him, a drop of burning oil fell from her lamp upon his shoulder.

The young god started up with a cry. 'Oh, foolish, curious Psyche,' he said, 'did I not warn you? Parting must be your punishment.' With these words he spread his wings and flew out of the window. Psyche threw herself on the ground in despair. The rule she had broken was real in many parts of the world. It survives still in the veil a bride wears at her wedding, and to break it then meant the end of happiness. Too late Psyche wept for her lost husband. No mortal dared give her shelter for fear of jealous Aphrodite, and the very beasts pitied her tears.

A white gull flew to Aphrodite, where she was bathing her

The Tasks of Psyche

fair body in the ocean. 'Cupid, your son, is married,' it squawked. 'Is his wife a goddess?' cried proud Aphrodite. 'Is she a nymph? or one of the Muses?' 'She is a mortal girl called Psyche,' answered the gossiping gull. 'Psyche, the stealer of my beauty!' cried Aphrodite in a towering rage. 'I shall find that wretched girl and punish her as she deserves!' She locked Cupid up and sent out heralds offering one of her kisses as a reward to anyone who would capture Psyche. After that every man in the world hunted the poor girl and at last one dragged her by the hair before the angry goddess. Aphrodite laughed scornfully. 'You have come to visit your husband, have you, ugly girl?' she said. 'Do you plan to make the goddess of love a grandmother? Then I shall treat you like a daughter indeed!'

The goddess poured baskets of wheat, barley, poppy seeds, grains of mustard, peppercorns and thistledown, all in one huge heap on the floor. 'Sort them out neatly, and let it be done before nightfall!' she said, and flounced off to a banquet. Psyche sat weeping on the floor, not even attempting the hopeless task. But an ant in a cranny had heard everything and called all her friends. 'Quick you children of Earth, the mother of us all, whether goddesses, girls or creeping creatures. Take pity on this poor child and help her!' Out came the ants in swarms and scurried to and fro over the flagstones with their burdens. Long before nightfall all the seeds lay in orderly heaps. 'This is not the work of your hands,' cried Aphrodite angrily when she saw it, and locked Psyche up for the night with a crust of bread.

Next morning she pointed out a flock of fierce sheep with sharp horns, grazing by the river bank. 'Fetch me some of their wool,' she ordered. Psyche was frightened, but a green reed sang to her in the wind. 'Rest here by me under this cool willow tree until the sheep have fallen asleep; then you may go safely and gather their wool where it has caught on the bushes and briars.' So Psyche filled her apron with tufts of wool and carried it back to Aphrodite, who laughed sourly and said, 'We shall soon see if you are as brave as you seem.' Next day she gave Psyche a crystal flask and told her to fetch water from the source of the dark river Styx. Psyche searched and found a great rock gushing bitter black water. On either side sleepless dragons stretched out their necks to seize her if she came near. As usual, Psyche could not think what to do, so sat down and cried. But a passing eagle took the bottle from her, and swooping through the black spray of the waterfall, filled it at the source and returned it to her again. Psyche hurried back to her cruel task-mistress, nursing the precious flask.

'You must be a witch!' cried Aphrodite angrily, 'but I will find you a harder task. Take this box down to the underworld and ask Persephone to spare me a little of her beauty. Mine is all worn out in nursing my son, so cruelly burnt by you, impudent girl!' 'This is the end of all,' thought Psyche, looking at the elegant box. 'I shall never return from the kingdom of death. Better to die swiftly, now.' She climbed a tower, meaning to throw herself down as the quickest way to death. But the tower heard her childlike sobs and spoke in its grave, marble voice. 'Psyche, take two halfpence in your mouth and three honey cakes in your hand, and go to the dark cave which leads to the underworld. Give the halfpenny to the boatman to ferry you across and the honey cakes to the dog with three heads that barks by the gate, to stop his mouths. Do not sit down in the underworld, or eat, or you must stay there. Persephone will give you her beauty and you may return the same way. Above all, do not look in the box!'

So Psyche did all that the tower commanded. She knelt at the feet of grave Persephone and received the magic secret of her beauty in the box. She came back the same way that she went, but once in the lovely light of day, she felt a longing to look inside the box. First she would; then she would not; then she longed to see the secret. Psyche was really not very clever. In the end she could not resist her curiosity, and lifted the lid. Instantly, spell-binding sleep rose from the box and spread round her in a cloud. She fell to the ground in a swoon and lay as if dead.

Meanwhile Cupid's burn had healed and he escaped from his jealous mother's palace, searching everywhere for Psyche. Flying overhead, he saw Psyche lying senseless on the ground beside the open box. With a sweep of glorious wings he landed

The Tasks of Psyche

by her. 'Poor precious Psyche,' he said, 'your curiosity will be the death of us both, yet I cannot bear to live without you.' Tenderly he wiped the sleep from her childish eyes, and breathed warm life into her body. Then he left her resting, while he flew up to Olympus to seek the help of Zeus.

Zeus called the gods together in council. 'You all know Cupid,' he said, 'for he has ranged the world making you all fools in love. Me, he has made turn myself into fire, birds and beasts to gain my desire. I, for one, would rather Cupid married a pretty mortal and stayed at home! I will make Psyche immortal, and Aphrodite's grandchildren shall be gods.' Aphrodite would have liked to sulk, but she was forced to agree, even to being a grandmother. So Hermes fetched Psyche to the shining floor of the sky's palace, and Zeus gave her immortality to drink. All the gods came to the marriage feast of Cupid and Psyche; the Hours decorated the hall, the Muses sang, Pan played his pipes, and even Aphrodite danced. So they were married and lived happily ever after," concluded the story-telling grandmothers. For, from the beginning of time, this was the only right and proper way to end a fairy tale.

Greeks and Trojans

Achilles kills Hector

On a lonely plain at the mouth of the Black Sea stood the city of Troy, with its high walls and towers commanding the way to Asia. The north wind shrieked round it at night, but within its walls lay heaped-up treasure, crowns, chains, buckles, bracelets and rings of pure gold. In Troy ruled old King Priam and his queen Hecuba, with many sons and daughters. Among the sons were Hector, tamer of horses, brave in battle, and handsome Paris, a favourite of Aphrodite, the golden-haired goddess of love. The city stood magnificent and powerful on the plain, but the will of the gods was that Paris should bring it to ruin. Aphrodite put it into his head to desire Helen, the most beautiful woman in the world. She had been courted by every prince in Greece and was married to Menelaus king of Sparta. But Paris seduced her, carried her on board a ship and took her to Troy, where she lived as his wife, spinning dark violet wool upon her golden spindle. By this theft Paris brought doom to Troy.

All the princes and chieftains of Greece gathered together their armies, and set out by thousands in their long ships across the sea to bring Helen back to her husband. Among them sailed many heroes of the Greeks: giant Ajax, wily

Odysseus, and Achilles, the great general from the mountains of the north, with his fierce fighting men, the Myrmidons. None knew what dangers they would meet before the gods allowed them to sail home again.

After many days they ran their ships ashore on the coast of Troy, where Hector waited with his troops drawn up in battle order. The fight was fierce, but the Greeks made a beach-head on the shore, from which they ravaged the coast. Hector, so proud and fearless, would never surrender a city which it was his duty to defend. Every day he went out from the huge gates of Troy to do battle with spear and sword against the round shields of the Greeks.

The gods looked down from high Olympus and saw all that happened. Often they too joined in the war. Aphrodite defended Troy, for handsome Paris was her favourite. With her went the war god, who was in love with her, and inventive Apollo. But to the Greeks at their ships went Hera and far-seeing Athena.

So for nine years the battle of gods and men swayed back and forth across the plain between Troy and the sea. Many hundred Greeks and Trojans were slaughtered as the years wore away and Troy was still not conquered. Then a quarrel over a captive woman broke out between Agamemnon, overlord of all the Greeks, and Achilles their best general. Achilles swore he would fight no more, and went back to the shore, where he sat in his tent, nursing his black and bitter rage among the ships. This quarrel was almost death to the Greeks. For the mother of Achilles, the silver-footed sea-nymph, Thetis, took her son's part, and begged Zeus to avenge him. Then Zeus sent a message telling Hector to attack the Greeks.

The high gates of Troy swung open, and into the plain poured the armies of the Trojans. They fell upon the Greeks, first with a hail of spears and arrows, then hand to hand, wrestling, trampling, swinging axes, slippery with sweat and blood. The chariots rolled forward, driving their sharp bronze prows against the enemy. Hector fought like the war-god himself, hurling rocks it would have taken two other men to lift. The attack drove the Greeks almost into the sea. In this

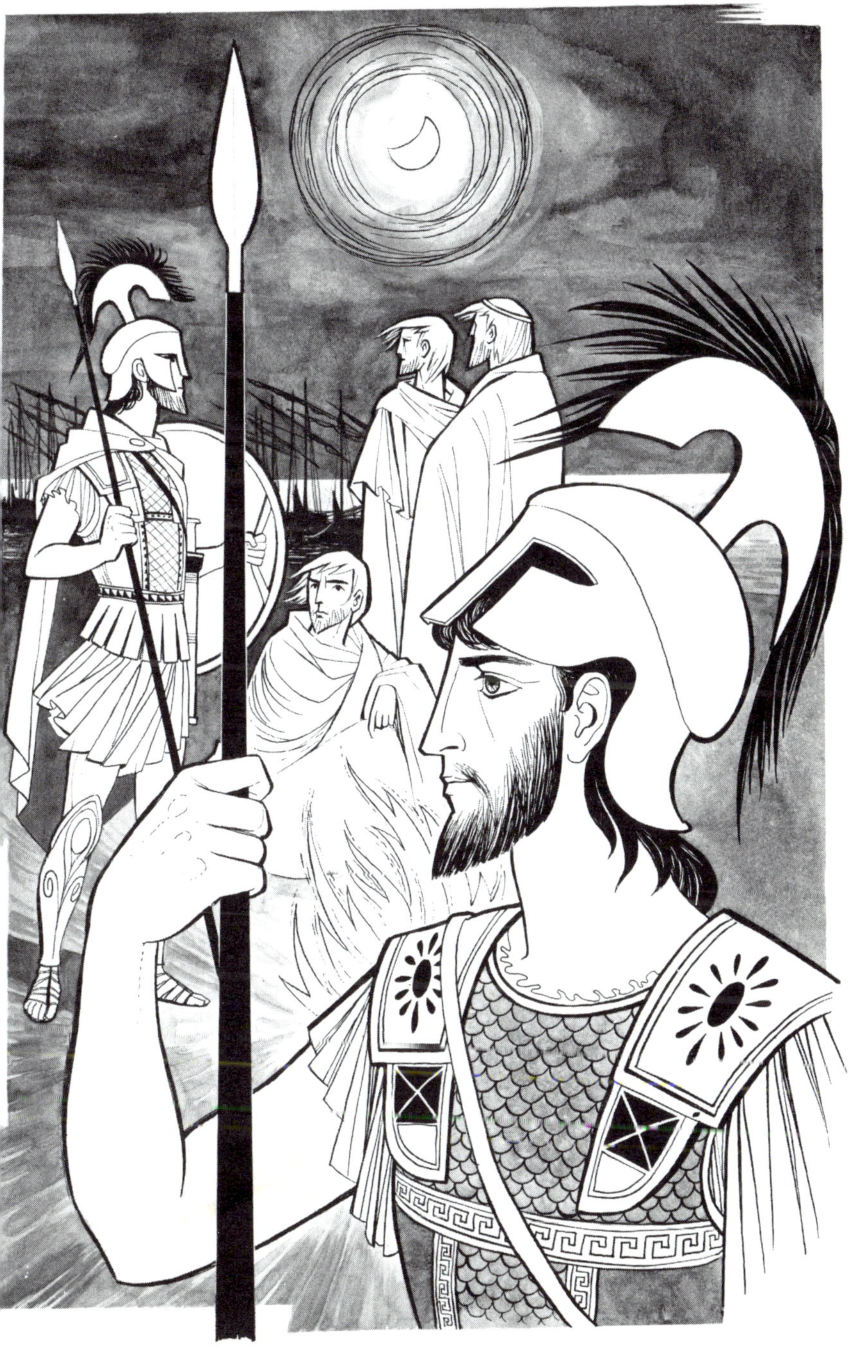

crisis, Patroclus, the beloved comrade whom Achilles loved more than any woman, begged to borrow his armour and lead the Myrmidons, not knowing that what he begged for was his own death. He fought all day like a mountain lion in courage, and the Trojans, seeing his armour, believed that Achilles had returned to fight. They wavered, turned and fled within their walls once more. But in the fight Hector stabbed Patroclus to death and stripped him of his borrowed armour.

When Achilles heard his friend was dead, he flung himself down in the dust, pouring ashes on his bright hair in the ritual of mourning. All night he mourned, refusing sleep or food. "I will go to find Hector, the slayer of my friend," he swore. "After that, let death come to me quickly." Thetis begged from the blacksmith god a new suit of armour for her son. Wearing its shining breastplate and crest of gold, Achilles set out to kill Hector and avenge his friend. The gods came down from Olympus, some on one side, some on the other, to take their part in this last battle.

Now the end drew near. The two armies clanged together with terrible thunder. The towers of Troy trembled and the ship masts of the Greeks shook like reeds in the wind. Achilles, with fury in his heart, searched the battle for Hector. For some time he was cheated by Apollo, who put on Trojan shape and drew him away from the battle. The Trojans retreated into the city and Apollo laughed. "Look!" he said. "The Trojans have escaped you." Achilles was furious. "You have made a fool of me!" he shouted at the god. He swerved and ran back towards Troy like a powerful racehorse, his breastplate shining bright as the dog-star in the sun. And Fate, for her own cruel purpose, kept Hector standing outside the city gate, alone.

Old Priam standing on the walls saw the danger his son was in and begged him to come in to safety. "Do not fight Achilles alone," he cried. "He is savage and has already robbed me of too many sons. Come inside the walls and do not throw your life away, for without you to protect me I shall be slaughtered, and the dogs I have fed at my own table will lick up my blood." Hecuba, too, cried out to her son, but Hector would not yield.

He stood firm, resting his bronze shield on a bulwark and

Achilles kills Hector

watching the monstrous Achilles bear down on him. "I have lost the battle," he said to himself, "and I cannot face my countrymen if I do not meet Achilles and either kill or be killed." Now Achilles was upon him, blazing like the god of war or the rising sun in his bright armour, raising his terrible spear to strike. Hector broke away from him, turned and ran, hoping to exhaust him. Achilles was after him in a flash. He ran like a falcon swooping after a pigeon that twists and turns in its flight. So Hector fled for his life from Achilles. Past the lookout, past the windswept fig tree they ran, past the spring and the stone trough where the Trojan wives and daughters used to wash their clothes in the peaceful days before the Greeks came. They circled three times round the walls of Troy with Hector in front and Achilles hard on his heels. They ran like champions in a race; but in this race the prize was the life of Hector.

All the gods watched in silence. Then Zeus sighed. "Hector is a good man and very dear to me. I wish I could save him from the hands of Achilles." Athena, who favoured the Greeks, was angry at these words. "The man is mortal," she said, "and his time has come." "It is true," answered Zeus sadly. "Do to him as you will." Then Zeus took the golden scales of judgement. In one balance he put the life of Hector, in the other the life of Achilles and Hector's side sank down towards Hades. Athena at once darted to the Trojan plain, disguised herself as Hector's brother and urged him to stand and fight. "Let us kill or be killed," called Hector to Achilles. "If I kill you I swear to respect your body and give it to your friends to bury. Will you do the same to me?" "No promises between sheep and wolves!" answered Achilles savagely. "You shall pay for all my pain and grief when you killed my friend."

With these words he hurled his great spear. Hector ducked and it flew over his head, to land quivering in the ground, where watchful Athena returned it unseen to Achilles. "You missed me!" shouted Hector. "Now may this spear of mine be buried in your body." He hurled it with all his might, but the spear fell blunted from Achilles' massive, god-wrought shield. Now Hector called to his brother for another spear, but found no brother there at his side to help him in the hour of need. He heard the mocking laughter of Athena and knew the goddess of the Greeks had tricked him. "The gods have led me to my death," thought Hector. "At least I can go to meet it bravely and children still unborn will read how Hector died."

He drew his sharp, heavy bronze sword from its belt and swooped, like an eagle from black clouds, on his enemy. Achilles, mad with savage anger, rushed to meet him, shield on guard, glittering spear poised to strike, plumes tossing on the golden helmet a god had made. Eyes narrowed, he searched the body of Hector for the place to strike, and saw the armour covered all but one opening, over the gullet. At this point Achilles aimed and with a powerful thrust he drove the spear clean through the throat. It was a mortal wound. Hector fell in the dust and Achilles straddled him in triumph.

"You stripped the armour from my friend Patroclus," he said, "and thought you would live to wear it. But now the dogs will maul your body, while we bury Patroclus with military honours." "I beg you," said Hector, as though to a brother-in-arms," do not throw my body to the dogs, but give it to my own people for burial." "You dog," said Achilles savagely, "I could almost cut your body to pieces and eat it raw for what you did to me." Hector was now on the point of death. "I know you," he said. "Your heart is hard as iron. I was wasting my breath. But the gods will remember, when your turn comes to die, how you treated me." Death cut him short. The soul left his body and sank to the house of Hades, leaving youth and manhood behind.

Achilles pulled out his spear and stripped off the blood-stained armour. The other Greeks came running and stood around, looking at the tall, magnificent body. They hacked at it with grim jests. "It is easy to fight with Hector now he is dead!" they shouted. Then Achilles did a fearful thing. He slit Hector's ankles and tied the tendons with leather thongs to his own chariot wheels. Then he whipped up his horses and drove off in a cloud of dust. Behind him dragged Hector's proud body, the dark hair trailing backwards on the earth, the face once so handsome, battered and torn by sharp stones.

All this old Priam and Hector's mother watched from the city walls, with bitter cries of grief. Hector's wife heard them from her distant room and came running. When she saw her husband's body dragged at Achilles' chariot wheels, she fell to the ground in a black swoon. All the women of Troy wept for her grief. So fate allowed the body of brave Hector to be defiled, before the eyes of his own people and on the very soil which had given him birth.

The Wooden Horse of Troy

AFTER the death of Hector the Greeks expected to take Troy. Yet still the remaining sons of Priam fought bravely and the city would not yield. New allies came to help the Trojans: an army of ten thousand splendid black Ethiopians and another of bare-breasted Amazon women on swift horses. The great Achilles himself was killed in the fighting by cowardly Paris. He would much rather have died at the hands of a brave Amazon woman, but the gods willed otherwise. When Achilles was born his mother had dipped him in the black waters of the river Styx, after which nothing could wound him. But she held the child by one heel, which remained his one fatal weak spot. Now garlanded Apollo himself guided an arrow to Achilles' heel, where it brought infection and death. The Greeks burnt his body and all that remained of the unconquerable Achilles, terror of the Trojans, was a handful of dust, hardly large enough to fill an urn. Now the Greeks swore the total surrender and destruction of Troy. Even if fair Helen had been given back to them, they would have fought on to avenge their dead. Ten years had passed, yet still the war dragged on.

It was Odysseus, whose home was under the clear skies of

The Wooden Horse of Troy

Ithaca, a man of winged cunning, who at last made the plot by which Troy fell. He beat himself till his body showed bruises like an ill-treated slave, put on filthy rags and slunk into Troy disguised as a beggar. He prowled through the streets gathering information like a master-spy. No one raised the alarm. Only one person recognized him, and that was the beautiful Helen herself. But she had suffered a change of heart. She was homesick for her own country and bitterly regretted the love affair with Paris, which had cost the lives of so many brave men. So Helen swore not to give Odysseus away, and helped him to escape to the Greek camp by the ships. Odysseus returned with a daring plan. He ordered a master-craftsman who served with the army to build a huge wooden horse with a concealed trap-door in its belly. Athena, helper of craftsmen, guided the maker's hand. The horse's head and hooves were perfectly carved, its hollow body large enough to hold twenty armed men. Some have said this so-called horse was a wooden siege-tower, but no true Greek believes them.

At night, when darkness hid everything, Odysseus and a picked band of comrades put on their fighting armour. They buckled on bronze breast-plates and shin-guards, took sword, shining shield and helmet, with frowning face-piece, and climbed a rope ladder into the belly of the wooden horse. The maker closed the cunning trap-door after them. Then the whole Greek army set fire to their brushwood huts, embarked in their ships and sailed away with noisy shouts. They went only to an island twelve miles off shore, but they were out of sight. When the Trojans looked out from their watch towers in the morning, the Greek camp was deserted, the grass trampled, the camp fires black, the huts burnt out. Wine skins and cooking pots littered the ruined camp and there was not a ship in sight. And there, before their gates stood the towering horse of wood. Its painted eyes shone, its nostrils gleamed redly, its stiff mane bristled with unravelled rope. The Trojans rushed to surround it with loud, excited arguments. "Pierce its sides with a bold stroke of the spear," shouted one. "No! Drag it to the heights and hurl it down on the rocks," shouted another. "Drag it into the city as an offering to the gods who have given us the victory," cried a third. "Never trust the Greeks," said the wise priest, Laocoon, "least of all when they pretend to give one gifts. There may be armed men inside!" To prove his point, the priest hurled a spear, which struck the wooden flanks with a groan, and stood quivering at the shock.

All this the Greeks hidden inside heard, without daring to speak. They could not even move, for fear their shields would clash. Worse was to follow, for lovely Helen came out of the gates to look at the wooden horse. Three times she went round it, touching the planks with slender fingers. Perhaps homesickness or some spirit of mischief possessed this calamitous woman, for she called out the names of the Greek captains one by one, even imitating the tender voices of their own wives. The Greek men had been ten years away from their women. It was all they could do not to leap up and answer her. One of them instinctively opened his mouth to reply, but Odysseus promptly clapped his hand over the man's face, until Athena prevailed on Helen to go away. By this piece of quick thinking Odysseus saved the entire plan.

The Greeks had left behind a well-briefed secret agent, Sinon. This man gave himself up to a patrol of Trojan soldiers, pretending to be a deserter. He said Odysseus had threatened to slaughter him as a sacrifice and begged the Trojans to take him in. As he told this pack of lies, he wept what looked like real tears, and the Trojans, who were simple honourable fighting men, believed him. Sinon worked on them. "The Greeks made the horse as an offering to their goddess Athena," he said. "If you destroy it she will surely destroy you. But if you bring it into the walls with honour she will protect your city and fight on your side." "Why is it so large?" asked old King Priam, feeling obscurely that something was wrong. "Why," answered Sinon readily, "that was the cunning of the Greeks. They built the horse big so that you should not be able to get it inside the gates and win the goddess's favour."

Athena herself helped the Greeks with ruthless cruelty. Laocoon, the wise priest and physician, who had warned the Trojans, went with his two young sons to sacrifice on the sea shore. He was in the act of drawing back the bullock's head to cut its throat before the altar, when two huge serpents swam in from the sea. They writhed towards the shore, churning the waves into foam, and reared their blood-red crests to look around. Then they gathered themselves like springs and fell on the two boys with flickering tongues and hissing jaws. The priest ran to help his children, but the snakes swiftly enfolded him in scaly coils, throttling the life from his body. The Trojans fled, pale with terror, leaving three lifeless bodies on the shore. The two snakes, glittering in evil triumph, glided away to sanctuary in the temple of Athena.

The question was now settled. Heaving on ropes and sweating, with rolling logs the Trojans dragged the wooden horse into their walled city. Their foolish songs and shouts of triumph drowned the clash of armed men inside. Three times the horse stuck in the very gates of Troy, but they even knocked down part of the wall with battering-rams to let it in. They forgot how long the huge stones had sheltered them and their children. For it was the will of Zeus that this proud city which had sunk a thousand ships and defied an army of heroes for ten years, should fall at last by trickery. It seemed as though the Trojans could hardly wait to destroy themselves. They spent the rest of the day feasting and drinking, convinced that they had won the war. They hung the horse with garlands of fresh leaves and decorated the streets by hanging their best rugs out of the windows. They danced and sang till they were worn out, then flung themselves down and snored. No sentries manned the walls, and even the chained watchdogs gnawing on unaccustomed bones forgot to bark.

Now silently, with muffled oars, the whole Greek fleet rowed back by moonlight to the shore they knew so well. A torch gave the signal to Sinon on shore. He lit an answering torch to show the coast was clear, stole to the wooden horse, where it stood huge and staring in the moonlit market-place, and softly drew the well-oiled bolts. One by one, the Greek captains climbed out with drawn swords. Silently they worked their way through the city, cutting the throats of sleeping guards and unbarring the massive gates. The main Greek army had crossed the windy plain for the last time and stood in silent battle order outside the town waiting for them. Troy was theirs.

A shout rang out in the dark, echoing from street to street, bringing death to the silent citadel. Before the Trojans could stumble out of bed and grope for their armour, before they could even think of defending themselves, the Greek host hurtled on its way. Men swept in through the wide-flung gates of Troy, hacking and burning as they went. The tall towers crumbled in ruins under their battering rams. Flames shot up to the sky, women shrieked as they were dragged from their burning houses. Their screams were lost in the clang of armour and angry battle yells. The ten years pent-up fury of the Greeks raged like a fire among standing corn or a flood that sweeps forests away. They butchered old Priam, as he had foretold, on the steps of his own palace. They killed the little son of Hector and made the Trojan women slaves. They killed white-haired old men in the streets and little children in their beds. Even in disaster men love life still, for they love its hopes, but the Trojans had nothing left to hope for. The Greeks, drunk with anger and victory, burnt even the temples of their gods.

In ten long years of war at Troy, hatred had bred hatred and death, death. Of the great city only mounds of rubble and rock remained, with sea birds wheeling in the empty sky above. Slowly the grass grew over the ruins and for nearly two thousand years they lay lonely and forgotten beside the sea, on the windy plain of Troy.

The Cyclops' Cave

Of all the Greeks who went to capture Troy, the boldest and wiliest was Odysseus, prince of Ithaca. No one could talk better than he, wrestling with thoughts, making words come to grips, never thrown by the tallest tale. The whole world knew of his clever tricks and the wooden horse with which he captured Troy. Yet ten years after the war was over, when all the other Greeks had returned to their cities, fate still left Odysseus roaming the high seas. He had offended Poseidon, lord of the waters, who sent one after another monsters, giants, enchantresses and tempests to bar his way. Only the friendship of clear-eyed Athena and the ready wit she gave him carried Odysseus home through adventures such as these.

At evening Odysseus and his men beached their curved ship, with its staring eye painted on the prow, to ward off the evil eye of fate. They had come to an island where they killed wild goats, grilled meat on spits at the camp fire, wrapped themselves in their faded, tattered travelling cloaks and lay down to sleep. When they woke next morning they saw across the water a land of bare hills and limestone cliffs, studded with caves. From the slopes came the sound of gruff voices and the bleating of many goats. From the caves they saw the smoke of wood fires drifting upwards. Odysseus rowed across to the mainland with twelve of his best men, carrying a skin of his finest wine, dark red, honeyed and potent.

They climbed to the first cave, a deep archway in the rock, overhung with ferns. There was a smell of sheep, of wood smoke and of country cheese. Outside, someone had built a yard, with rough dry-stone walls, to shelter his flock at night. But the owner of the cave was nowhere to be seen. They searched and shouted among the echoing rocks, but no one answered. He was out, guarding his sheep on the high pastures, among the bitter wild thyme and the shrilling grasshoppers. The men grew bolder. One by one they went into the cave and looked around at the baskets of cheese and the bowls of buttermilk set on the stone floor to cool.

"Let us hope the master of this cave will prove a friendly host," said Odysseus. They took these words for a hint, lit a fire from the embers on the hearth, killed a young lamb from the pen, took down a basket of goats' cheese and feasted. They were just finishing their meal when there was a sound of heavy footsteps outside. A flock of fat sheep crowded into the cave. Behind them came their shepherd, whom at first the men could not see, for he had heaved a huge stone over the doorway. He lit a fire, sat down to milk his sheep and goats by the light of the flames and then caught sight of Odysseus. "Strangers," he bellowed, "and who may you be?" At the roar of his voice their hearts sank. He was one of the Cyclopes, banished by Zeus to the fiery mountain. His name was Polyphemus. He was three times the size of mortal man. In the centre of his forehead was one great staring eye, and above it ran a shaggy black eyebrow, which now frowned upon them. But Odysseus, ever ready of speech, stepped forward and greeted this monster politely. "Sir," he said, "we are travellers driven out of our way by a storm. Necessity forces us to be your guests, and we hope you will remember all guests are sacred to a god-fearing man."

For answer to this diplomatic speech, the Cyclops reached out a huge hand and picked up two of the sailors at once. He

The Cyclops' Cave

swung them by their heels, dashed their heads upon the floor till their brains ran out over the stones. Then he tore them to pieces and swallowed them, entrails and all, washing down his meal with great draughts of goats' milk. The others watched, too terrified to speak, too terrified almost to pray to Zeus, the travellers' god, for his protection. After his supper of human flesh, the Cyclops lay down to sleep among his flocks. Soon his giant snores shook the cave, while the men huddled together in misery and waited for the morning.

As soon as dawn reddened the eastern sky the Cyclops got up, milked his ewes and lit a fire. He snatched up two more of the company, crammed them into his mouth for breakfast and swallowed them before the eyes of their comrades. Then he rolled away the stone from the cave mouth and drove his flock out to graze. But before he followed them he heaved the huge stone back, imprisoning the Greeks. With murder in their hearts they heard his heavy footfall die away into the distance. Four strong men could not have shifted the stone that the Cyclops rolled as easily as a pebble.

The men in the cave gave themselves over to lamenting and despair until Odysseus silenced them. "Men of Ithaca," he began, "hear my plan. While the Cyclops can see us, he will never let us escape. We must take this walking stick, large as a ship's mast, which he has left in the cave. We must sharpen its point and harden it in the embers of the fire. Then you may cast lots among you, to help me drive it into his single eye, while he lies sleeping. When he is blinded we can surely escape him." The men groaned and argued, as Greeks will, but agreed. There was nothing else to be done.

Evening came and with it Polyphemus returned driving his shaggy flock before him into the cave. When his milking was done he snatched up two more of the party, and opened his vast mouth to swallow them. But Odysseus stepped forward, courteous and disarming, holding in his hands a wooden bowl of the strong, dark wine. The Cyclops snatched the bowl and drained it at a gulp. "Give me more wine, stranger," he said, licking his chops. "And tell me your name." Three times Odysseus filled the bowl and three times the giant emptied it.

Then when he saw that the wine had befuddled Polyphemus's wits, Odysseus answered him. "My name is Nobody; that is what all my friends call me, Nobody." The Cyclops gave a loud laugh. "Nobody! What a name! Then of all your company I will eat Nobody last and the rest before him." Then he fell backwards on the floor in a drunken sleep and lay there snoring.

Silently the Greeks set the olive-wood staff in the fire to heat, silently four of them together poised it above the Cyclops's head and drove it home in his one great eye. The Cyclops gave a terrible scream, which echoed through the cave, and they backed away in horror as he pulled the stake from his bleeding eye-socket and hurled it from him, howling. His cries re-echoed through the mountain and the earth shook as the other Cyclopes came running from their caverns. "What is it, Polyphemus? Why are you shouting? Is it robbers attacking you?" "Oh no, my brothers," he bellowed. "It is Nobody! Nobody is killing me!" When they heard this the Cyclopes shrugged their huge shoulders. "If nobody is killing you, why do you wake us all up with your bellowing?". And grumbling they stumped off to their beds of dried leaves, while Odysseus laughed secretly at the success of his cunning trick.

Yet the Greeks were still not out of danger. How were they to escape from the cave, while Polyphemus in blind rage sat in the doorway with arms outstretched waiting to clutch them? Plan after plan, trick after trick passed through Odysseus's wily mind. Finally deep in the cave he seized the sheep and bound them together in threes with ropes of twisted withies. Then under each group he bound one of his men. He himself chose the leader of the flock, a splendid ram with spiral horns and glowing yellow eyes. Ducking under its shaggy belly, he clung to it, twisting his hands in the thick, soft fleece. Thus, for the second time the Greeks waited for the dawn.

At sunrise, as the black shadow of the windy headland ran back across the sea, the sheep smelt the grass and began to bleat. Polyphemus rolled aside the stone and let them out. The great ram, burdened with Odysseus, came last. The Cyclops felt it closely. "Why are you last, dear ram," he groaned, "you

The Cyclops' Cave

who always led your ewes so proudly? Are you grieved for your poor master, blinded by that wicked Nobody?" Odysseus shrank into himself, and at last the giant let the ram through. Outside Odysseus slipped from under its belly and untied his men. Together they drove the fine flock down to the boat, where their comrades, who had given them up for dead, welcomed them with joy.

They bundled the fat sheep on board and pulled on their oars until they had put the water between themselves and the land of the Cyclops. Then Odysseus stood up in the stern and shouted. "Cyclops, you thought you were too strong for us, but we were not so feeble after all. Now the gods have punished you as you deserve for making a meal of your own guests!"

These taunts enraged the blind Cyclops, who tore off a jagged lump of rock and hurled it in the direction of the mocking voice. The rock fell into the sea with a mighty splash, raising a wave that almost swept them back to land. Again Odysseus shouted, grown reckless with triumph, and another great rock landed alongside. For the third time Odysseus stood up and cupped his hands around his mouth, so that his voice carried across the water. "Cyclops, if anyone asks you who put out your eye, tell him it was the sacker of cities, Odysseus of Ithaca!" With a last shout of rage, the Cyclops heaved up a whole hillock and flung it after them. This time it fell short and the wave it raised swept them on safely to the island shore. There Odysseus feasted, offering the splendid ram which had carried him to safety in thanksgiving to Zeus.

Then the Greeks sailed away on their journey. But the three rocks which fell into the sea stand there in the shadow of Mount Etna to this day. Smoke still rises from caves in the mountain as though from giant cooking pots. And the people of the island say that when the volcano glows on dark nights you may still see the one red eye of Polyphemus.

The Enchantress's Palace

ANOTHER landfall after storms and dangers brought Odysseus and his men to a land of thick forests. For two days and nights they lay on the beach, too exhausted to move. The third morning brought a lovely dawn. Odysseus rose up, left his crew sleeping and struck boldly inland. He made his way by winding paths through the forest to a rocky hill, and there, shading his eyes from the glare, he looked around. He saw at once that they were on an island, ringed to the horizon by sun-polished sea. There was no sound but the beating of waves on the shore and the ceaseless conversation of doves in the forest. Near at hand everything was hidden by thickets of scrub oak, but in the distance a wisp of wood smoke rose above the trees.

Odysseus shot a deer, dragged it back to the ship and woke his men who still lay sleeping with heads muffled in their cloaks. When they had all feasted and drunk from their wineskins, he told them what he had seen. The men began to sob and groan, convinced that the island was the home of another monster which would devour them all. "My friends," said Odysseus, who never lost his head, "we are not dead yet, though if we stay here on the beach we shall starve. Let us make

The Enchantress's Palace

a workable plan." Unwillingly the men drew lots from a bronze helmet, and divided into two parties, commanded by Odysseus and his kinsman, Eurylochus. The lot fell to Eurylochus and his party to explore the island, while the others guarded the boat, which was their only means of escape. With bitter tears the men parted from their comrades and set out. They took the inland trail, now cool and dark under the trees, now hot in the sun, and presently came to a clearing in the forest. Before them stood a house, with lofty porch and pillars of carved stone.

As the men stood wondering, a pack of savage-looking wolves and lions rushed down the steps towards them. The men drew their swords, set their backs to the pillars of the house and made ready to defend themselves to the death. To their amazement, the beasts ran to them with wagging tails, licking their feet and hands and jumping up to reach their faces, like dogs to their master. The men climbed the steps, the animals still bounding around them, almost as though they were trying to speak. They stood in the open porch looking around them, when they heard a sound from within the hall. It was the clack of a weaver's shuttle travelling backwards and forwards across the loom and with it came the sound of a woman's lovely voice singing. "Men," said one of the captains, "there's someone working at a loom. Woman, nymph, or goddess, whatever she may be, let's give her a shout."

They hallooed noisily. The polished cypress doors of the great house were flung wide by unseen hands and Circe came out to greet them. She smiled strangely, and her beautiful hands beckoned them to follow her inside. They trooped into her high hall, rich with carving and tapestries. But cautious Eurylochus suspected a trap and stayed waiting outside. He sat there on the steps until evening, listening and calling, but no one answered him and not one of the men returned. All he could hear was the shrill squeal of pigs from the farm-yard behind the house. Choking with sobs the brave Eurylochus went back to the ship alone.

Meanwhile Circe led the men into her great hall and sat

them on the soft couches which lined the walls. Her waiting maids brought water and washed them with gentle hands. Then the banqueting tables were set before them, and Circe herself, with her fair hands, mixed bowls of barley-meal and honey, flavoured with wine. The men, enjoying almost-forgotten luxuries, did not see her add to each bowl a few drops of a powerful drug, but ate with smiles and courteous thanks. Circe was an enchantress, priestess of Hecate the witch-goddess. She had distilled the drug herself out of herbs from her secret witch's garden. When the bowls were empty and the men lay happy on their couches, she moved round the hall, striking them lightly one by one with the slender wand in her hand.

She laughed then to see the change that came over them. Their bodies bloated, their ears grew long, their eyes buried themselves in rolls of fat, bristles sprouted from their cheeks, their noses turned to mottled snouts, their hands to hooves, and when they tried to cry for help, their piteous words turned to the grunting and squealing of a herd of pigs. Stamping her foot contemptuously and whipping them with her wand, Circe drove them out on all fours to the pigsties of her farm. She flung them some handfuls of acorns and husks and left them there to wallow in the dirt.

At the ship, Odysseus questioned his cousin. When he heard the story—how the men had gone into the house with the beautiful woman and not one of them had reappeared—Odysseus slung his bow over his shoulder, took his bronze sword and set forth without more words. Odysseus was deep in the enchanted glades when he saw a young man in helmet and short travelling cloak, coming towards him as swiftly as if his feet had wings. In his hand he carried a herald's staff. It was, of course, Hermes, who now appeared as a handsome young mortal with crisply curling hair.

He smiled and shook Odysseus by the hand. "My poor Odysseus," he said, with his irresistible charm, "what are you doing wandering about in this most dangerous forest?" "I am looking for my friends," answered Odysseus. "Do you not know," said the gods' messenger, "that this is the island of

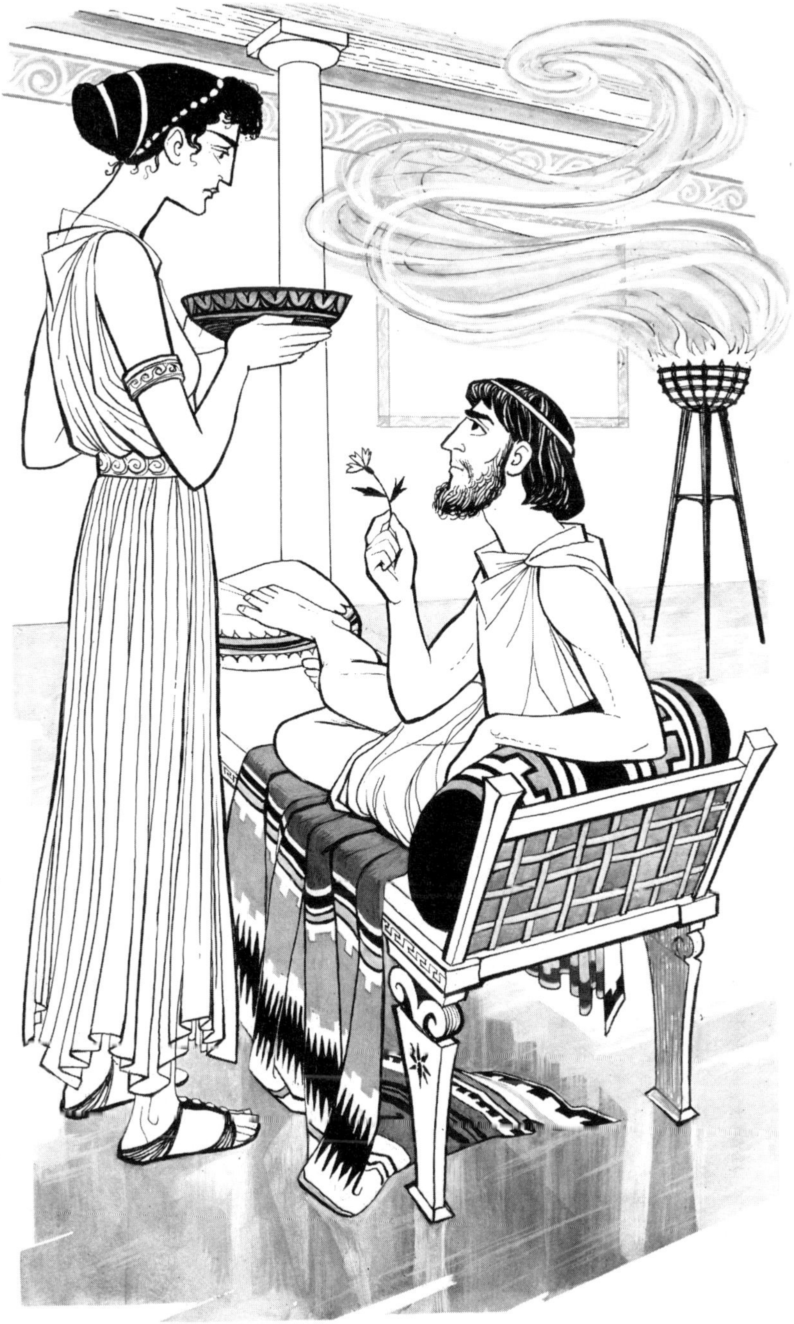

Circe, who has turned your friends by her black arts into pigs? She will try to do the same to you for her own amusement. But do not be afraid. I can give you a charm against her." He stooped and picked a flower, which he put in Odysseus's hand. It was the fabulous herb moly, with white petals, black root and magic power. "Hold this flower when Circe gives you her drugged wine to drink," said the god. "When she touches you with her wand, draw your bronze sword, as though you meant to kill her. She will shrink in terror, then she will try her other wiles and invite you to her bed. Make love to her, then make her swear by the gods not to try any more of her tricks." Odysseus turned to thank him, but the god had vanished. Thoughtfully he went on through the forest alone.

Outside the enchantress's palace, he kicked away the fawning lions and wolves which had once been men. He went boldly up the steps and knocked with the hilt of his sword on the polished doors. Circe came at once, charming in robe of airy gauze, a golden girdle round her waist. She led Odysseus herself with many soft words to a couch in the place of honour. Her maids set a low table before him and murmured softly as they offered him a bowl of drugged wine. The squealing and grunting of swine sounded fearfully loud from the back of the house.

Odysseus held the white moly flower tightly in one hand. With the other he took the bowl and drained it to the dregs. "Be off with you!" cried Circe sharply, striking him with her magic wand. "Be off to the pigsties and wallow with your friends." As Odysseus stood motionless, her face grew dark with anger and she repeated her command. For answer, Odysseus drew his sword and rushed at her. Instantly Circe changed her tactics. She slipped through his grasp like water, fell at his knees and began to sob. "What other man could swallow that drug and not suffer enchantment? You are the great Odysseus, the famous warrior whom nothing can defeat. Spare me, spare me I beg, for I love you. Love me and in love we will learn to trust each other. Believe me, I will be your faithful friend!" "Circe," replied the wily Odysseus, putting on his sternest look, "first you must promise to try no more of

The Enchantress's Palace

your tricks. Then set my men free and let me see them face to face."

With languishing looks, the enchantress led him through her great house and over the courtyard to the pigsties. She unlatched the doors and out came the pigs, rolling and grovelling in the dust, until Circe touched them with a secret salve. Then their pigs' hides dropped from them. They stood upright, younger, taller and handsomer than ever before, laughing and weeping at once for happiness. At first they could hardly believe themselves out of danger. Yet when they saw the timid sidelong glances which Circe threw towards Odysseus, and heard the gentle, almost frightened voice in which she spoke to him, they knew they were safe so long as he was there. Singing and shouting through the forest they went back to the ship, helped their comrades to stow the boat-gear in a cavern and all returned together to feast in Circe's hall.

The serving maids had been busy. One had spread fine-woven rugs over the couches. Another had drawn up silver tables set with golden baskets of fruit, while others were mixing bowls of spiced wine. The rest lit a log fire and heated water in a bronze cauldron on the hearth. They bathed the weary travellers and rubbed their bodies with scented oils. They gave them tunics of fresh linen, and fleecy cloaks from Circe's loom. When the men saw each other, so handsome in their true shapes, they could hardly speak. Soon all sat together round the hall. The cook lifted the hissing spits of grilled meat from the flames. Circe, terrible no longer, filled the drinking bowls with her own hands, and served them, smiling softly. It seems that, though a witch, she was truly in love with bold Odysseus. So the company feasted in the enchantress's palace and stayed with her for a whole year. When the year was out, for all her tears and wiles, they took ship again and after many more adventures, reached home at last.

Strange Shapes

The Pirate Ship

"THE gods wear many faces," wrote a Greek author, for they were masters of disguise. Zeus changed his shape to marry Hera at the beginning of the world. He shrank into a cuckoo on the mountainside and raised a bitter storm. Hera saw the bird shivering in the freezing rain and opened her cloak to shelter it in her warm lap. As she enfolded it, powerful arms seized her by the waist and the god took possession of her. Gods often spoke to men in the voice of birds, who fly so near them in the wide blue air. The cuckoo in the oak tree tells that Zeus will send the spring rain. The swallow skimming the stream reminds the farmer to prune his vines. The fates tell men their fortunes in the shape of magpies.

> One for sorrow,
> Two for mirth,
> Three for a wedding
> And four for a birth.

So country folk have read their message since time began. The gods live also in tendril and leaf. The laurels of Delphi speak Apollo's warning and the great rustling oak tree at Dodona whispers the commands of Zeus. Gods in search of love or sport walk the earth, sometimes as beasts. Zeus became a ram with curling horns, Hera a snowy cow, Artemis, the hunter, a wild mountain-cat, and Aphrodite a fish, swimming in the sea where she was born. No shape is too strange for them, not even snail the House-Carrier or ant the Wise One. Moreover they have the power to transform men, women, beasts, even wood and stone, at will. Peacocks, leopards, fountains, temples, islands, stars are scattered round the paths they have trodden. Here are some tales of strange shapes created by the gods.

Once a pirate galley from Tyre put into a lonely bay among the islands of Greece. The keel grated on the stones. The pirates leapt overboard with their waterskins and ran to fill them at a fresh-water stream which trickled down to the sea. Ill fate was their captain and they were a desperate crew, eagle-beaked, dark and scowling as Hades, quick as cats, murderers and robbers many of them, with a price on their heads. The only honest man among them was the steersman Acoetes, son of a poor fisherman, whom poverty alone had driven into their company. His father had died, saying, "Take all the riches I have, my skill and my craft." Acoetes, with the winds and the stars as his only inheritance, became pilot to this black crew. He left the ship now and climbed a high rock, to try the wind with a wetted forefinger, as sailors do, and search the sky for signs of a storm.

The sky was clear and the sea sparkled darkly like wine as he returned and saw on the shore a knot of men struggling, as though they were trying to overpower some wild beast. "Look here at this," cried one, and Acoetes saw a young boy, lovely and languid as a girl, whom his shipmates had found sleeping among the rocks. His eyes were still heavy with sleep or wine, his long dark hair hung tangled round his shoulders. He seemed hardly to hear or understand them. "Tie him up," shouted a sailor, and the lovely boy lay limp and still, while the mate ran for a coil of rope from his locker. Roughly, they twisted the prisoner's hands behind his back and began to bind them, but in spite of all their curses and their sailors' cunning with knots, the twisted ropes always untied themselves

The Pirate Ship

and fell to the ground, while their captive lay smiling at them, with dark, inscrutable eyes.

"Fools!" cried Acoetes."Do you not see there is some god within this lovely body? He will call up winds and storms. If we take him on board we are all dead men!" He straddled the gang-plank and would have barred the way, but the mate, who had been banished for a brutal murder, took him by the throat and held him half strangled, while the others dragged the prisoner on board. They flung him down on deck, and the boy spoke for the first time, drowsily, as if he were coming to his senses after drinking long and deep. "Where am I? Where are you taking me?" he asked. "We will take you wherever you want to go, my fine young gentleman," answered the captain craftily, smelling ransom. "Naxos, among the islands, is my home," murmured the strange boy. His eyelids drooped again, and he seemed to sleep, lying helpless among his garlands of vine and ivy leaves.

The captain shouted, the sailors swarmed nimbly up the mast to shake out sail, while Acoetes at the wheel set his course by the headland's point. The ropes snapped taut, the rigging groaned, the wind filled the sail in a proud arch, and the ship bounded over the sea towards Naxos. "You fool!" roared the captain. "We are not bound for Greece. Set your course eastward for Egypt. We can sell this pretty young fellow for many pieces of gold in the slave markets there." Knocking Acoetes aside, he took the helm himself, and put it hard over to the east.

Then the gods made sport of them. The ship kicked, swung prow out of water like a rearing horse, shuddered through all her timbers, then lay quivering in the swift-running sea, as still as if she were in dock. The sailors ran to their benches and tugged on the oars, but they could not shift her forward a foot. For suddenly, in an instant, so it seemed, a network of vines and ivy leapt up to imprison the enchanted ship. Ivy muffled the oars, ivy smothered the main mast in glossy leaves and dark fruit. A grape vine flung its thousand tendrils around the yard arms, the rigging sagged under the weight of purple grapes, the decks were knee-deep in boughs of golden fruit. Through the ship ran a stream of dark wine with madness rippling in its heady fumes.

The sailors rushed to look for a hiding place, for now they heard on all sides the snarling of wild beasts. There on the prow, glittering in the rays of the sun, stood the captive youth, grown now to more than mortal size, his head crowned with vine leaves, an ivy-wreathed wand in his hand. Swiftly he changed shapes before their terrified eyes. Now he was a lion roaring in the bows, now a shaggy mountain bear in the stern. Then he was a god again with blazing eyes, commanding the panthers and dappled leopards crouched by his side. His mouth, purple-stained with wine laughed at their terror, for he, their helpless captive, was Dionysus, god of the vine.

Now they understood his drugged sleep, his feminine beauty, the vine-leaves in his hair. For Dionysus, the child of Zeus, had been hidden from jealous Hera by his mother. She dressed him as a girl and sent him to be brought up by the nymphs in a secret, ivy-shadowed cave among the dells of Mount Nysa. Here he created wine, and wandered the hills with a wild company of nymphs and satyrs, reeling and shouting till the woods rang. Wine brings men dancing, singing and joy, but too much drives them mad. In their frenzy the worshippers of Dionysus tear beasts and men to pieces. He gave men wine for grief as well as joy. He is a lovely but a dreadful god.

Wild terror seized the pirate crew. The faithful helmsman, Acoetes, fell on his knees on deck. The others stumbled towards the stern, but fell back in terror when a snarling lion sprang up to meet them there and seized the captain in its jaws. In madness of terror, the mate flung himself over the gunwale and plunged into the sea, followed by all the crew. They hit the water with a splash and rose from the swirling salt foam as men no longer. Their bodies darkened, their backs arched, their arms shrank to fins, their legs to waving tails. They leapt and plunged in the waves like acrobats, blowing out spouts of water from their nostrils and dashing up clouds of spray from the blue sea.

Where there had been twenty men, a school of dolphins

The Pirate Ship

furrowed the waves, while all around them the thousand sons and daughters of Poseidon shook the sea with their godlike laughter. Alone of all the crew, Acoetes remained. Trembling with cold, half out of his mind with dread, he awaited the anger of the god. But Dionysus smiled, with strange immortal grace, and ordered him to steer for Naxos and fear nothing. There Acoetes discharged his sacred cargo, kindled a fire on the flat stones of the shore and offered sacrifices of thanksgiving. He learned the wild uproarious rites of the vine god, and like all the people in that land, worshipped Dionysus in a cup of wine.

King Midas

THERE was once a king of Lydia named Midas. Men said that this king's father had been a satyr, with the horns and shaggy hind-quarters of a mountain goat. Certainly he was a friend to satyrs. The young god Dionysus travelled through his land, crowned with vine leaves and followed by a band of satyrs, reeling drunk from potent dark wine. Drunkest of all was his tutor, old, bald, red-faced Silenus, who stumbled into the gardens of King Midas and sprawled snoring among his rose trees. The royal gardeners discovered him, bound him and dragged him before the king. Midas, who had tasted the joys of wine himself, recognized in this battered old reveller a chosen companion of the god, and entertained him with ten days of feasting, in which they drank deep together.

On the eleventh morning, as they saw the swimming stars grow pale in the sky, Midas with hiccoughing good-humour led Silenus, stout and swollen as his own wine-skin, back to the god. Dionysus was delighted to see his disreputable old schoolmaster. The young satyrs danced round, hanging him with chains of flowers. Even the leopards which drew the chariot of the god growled their contentment. "Choose yourself a gift," said Dionysus to Midas; "whatever you choose, it shall be given to you." Perhaps the king's wits were still fuddled with wine which makes fools of us all, for he answered without thinking, "Let everything I touch be turned to gold."

Dionysus thought he might have chosen more wisely, but he would not break his godlike word, and sent Midas off with this dangerous gift. The foolish king went home, hugging himself with the thought of how rich he would be. He could not wait to test the power of the god's magic. An oak tree grew beside the dusty chariot road, with one bough hanging down temptingly near his hand. Midas snapped a twig. Instantly the acorn glittered and the green leaves, trembling delicately in the light air turned to gold.

Midas was enchanted. He snatched up a stone from the road, breathless to see it glisten in the palm of his hand. A madness of greed swept through him like a summer fever, making his pulses hammer as he touched robes, sandals, chariot, everything within reach. The dust from the wayside dropped from his fingers in a golden rain, an ear of wheat shone, with every grain in jewelled perfection, as he plucked it. And when he picked a common red and green apple from a wayside tree, you would have sworn it came from the magic garden of the Hesperides, where the sun turns everything to gold as its sinks in the western sea. Midas hurried home to his palace and laid a greedy finger on the high pillars of the porch. Instantly they glittered in the morning air, brighter than Athena's temple. He called for water to wash, and all his servants gaped to see a shower of golden drops fall from his wet hands.

"A banquet to celebrate my riches!" cried Midas. The cook slaves scurried around the great courtyard, from bakehouse to open hearth or cool cellar. They roasted venison with subtle herbs, baked crusty loaves and piled the tables high with dishes of grapes and apricots. Midas stretched himself on his banqueting couch, turned, of course, to cloth-of-gold at his touch. He idly broke a piece of bread and frowned to feel it cold and hard in his hand. His mouth watered at the good smell of roast meat, but when his steward carved him a slice, his teeth bit on the sickening taste of metal. His butler poured a cup of the rich, dark wine he loved so well. "Surely", thought Midas to himself, "Dionysus will not change the gift of wine, which he himself created for man's pleasure!" Yet as it touched his lips he felt again the cold, hard, nauseous metal. By the end of the day the king was tortured with hunger and thirst and knew himself wretched in spite of all his riches.

Now Midas detested the wealth he had longed for. People took him as a proverb and said "rich as Midas", but he knew his gold had made him more wretched than the poorest peasant in his kingdom. He stretched out his arms in their hated golden sleeves towards the sky and prayed to Dionysus. "Save me, save me, Lord of the Vines, from this hateful gold which is killing me!"

Dionysus could not help smiling at this besotted mortal, but since he, among all the gods, is easy-going and good-humoured, he took pity on him. "Go to the river Pactolus which flows through your lands," he said. "Follow it upstream to the mountain, where it foams and bubbles from its spring among the rocks. Dive into the water and you will wash away your folly." How fresh and cold the mountain waterfall felt. What a cool breath rose from its clouds of spray! How blessedly the clear water washed the hateful gold from his hair and body. Ever afterwards the golden sands of that river were famous. The spring floods swept grains and nuggets of pure gold into the plain below and the whole kingdom grew rich from it.

As for Midas, he loathed riches and loved to wander in the woods, where Pan lives in his mountain cave. At evening, when Pan came out and played his pipes for the nymphs of the forest to dance, Midas would sit by under the pine trees, wagging his head in time with the music. It pleased him, for the shepherds of that hilly land were all pipers. Men even say it was the Lydians who taught the Greeks to play the wailing flute. One evening, as the dance broke up, and the nymphs sat laughing and breathless on the grass, shaggy Pan began to boast. "Not even Apollo, lord of musicians, can make better music than I with my hollow reeds," he said.

There was a sunburst, a brilliance like a star, and Apollo

stood among them. His hair crowned with laurel, streamed in the mountain wind, his purple robe swept the ground. He held the lyre his sure and skilful hands had made. Only an artist could stand as he did. "Let us both play," he said, and his voice itself was music. "The god of this mountain shall judge between us." The ancient god of the mountain came, shaking his head free of oak trees and smoothing his rustling green beard as he settled himself down in the glade.

The lovely nymphs sat down in a circle to listen, the whisper of their trees silent for once. Then Pan put his pipes of dried rushes to his lips and began to play a shepherd's dance. The wild goats on the mountain side leapt to hear it, the nymphs swayed in the rhythm of the dance, and Midas wagged his head from side to side in blissful enjoyment. The piping ceased. Apollo lifted the lyre, sweeping the strings with powerful, delicate fingers as he began to play. A hush fell; the very air stood still. The tall trees bowed their heads, tears ran down the cheeks of the lovely nymphs and even the old god of the mountain breathed a deep sigh as if something long forgotten had returned to his mind.

When the music ended he bowed to Apollo and all the nymphs nodded their heads in approval of his choice, too moved to speak. Suddenly the silence was broken by a voice, raucous and loud as a donkey braying. "You can keep the lyre," said stupid Midas. "Give me the pipes!" The company stood frozen, too frightened by the insult to the great god even to speak. But Apollo only laughed, and looked thoughtfully at Midas's head. "Poor Midas," he said, "He has ears no better than an ass." And he vanished, in a swirl of purple cloak, on his way to distant Olympus.

King Midas went home and was entering his palace when he was disturbed by an unaccountable twitching sensation on his head. At first he took no notice, but the twitching continued. He put up a hand to scratch his ear, and encountered something bristly and shaggy, which seemed to his terrified fingers to extend far above his head. He rushed to his innermost room, snatched up his looking glass of polished silver, then dropped it again with a howl. One glance was enough to show him a pair of long grey asses' ears flapping above his head. So he is always shown in pictures, though some people pretend he is only wearing a donkey mask, like a folk-dancing hobby-horse. To Midas they seemed real enough. He began to rummage through his treasure chests for something to hide the god's revenge, and after several attempts managed to imprison the wayward ears under a turban of purple silk. Turbans became the fashion at that eastern court and the secret was well hidden.

Yet there was one person from whom it could not be concealed—the royal barber. This slave came as usual next morning to shave his master. He began to unwind the turban, when, to his horror, a pair of long shaggy ears burst out and tickled him on the chin. The barber let out a cry of alarm. King Midas rounded on him with an anger that would have been terrible if it were not for the undignified wagging of those ears. "Swear to keep secret what you have seen!" he said. "If you breathe a word of this, your body shall be thrown to the dogs to eat." In terror the barber gave his word and went away to brood on what he had seen. The asses' ears of King Midas took possession of his slave's mind. Vast, grey, and shaggy they filled his waking thoughts. When he slept, they twitched and flapped in his dreams until the man began to fear he would go mad.

He dared not tell the royal secret, yet he could not bear to keep it any longer. One morning early, before anyone was about in the courtyards and streets, he went out and dug a deep hole by the highway. He lay down by it and put his head inside. "Do you know," he whispered to earth, "that King Midas has ears like an ass?" Then, with a sigh of relief, delivered from his obsession, he shovelled the earth over his secret and went back to bed. He did not know that already the seed was sown, and a thicket of rushes was thrusting its fists up through the dark earth.

Next spring King Midas walked in procession along the highway with all his court. His riches were still the world's fable. A jewelled canopy was held over his head, slaves fanned him with peacocks' feather fans, his head was bound with a turban of royal purple silk. As the procession drew near the place where the barber had whispered his secret, the courtiers saw a thicket of tall graceful reeds which grew where he had dug. A light wind blew, the reeds swayed and rustled, with a sound like many voices whispering softly. The rustling began to form words, eagerly picked up and passed from one listener to another. "Ss-ss-ss," the leaves were whispering, "King Midas has ears like an ass– like an ass– like an ass– like an ass-ss-ss."

The Country Cottage

SOMETIMES it pleased the gods on Mount Olympus to come down from their cloudy heights and visit the homes of men. So it happened one day that Zeus, the father of the gods, laid aside his thunderbolts, Hermes the messenger unbound his winged boots, and disguised as travellers they entered the city of Tyana in hilly Phrygia. They strolled through the streets, they went into temples, where sacrifices to the gods lay smoking on the altars. They stopped to listen by market stalls where traders haggled over the price of peppers and goats' cheese. Then, as the sun glared white in the midday sky, they began to look for a lodging where they could shelter from the heat.

The people of Tyana had forgotten that Zeus is the patron of travellers, and that all strangers asking hospitality come in his name. Door after door was banged and bolted in the two gods' faces, and chained watchdogs snarled at their tread. By noon the streets were empty. Everywhere the shutters were up. Even the dogs lay stretched out in the shade, and lizards on the scorching stones seemed to be the sole owners of the city. Then the two gods, hungry and thirsty, angry and tired, turned their backs on Tyana and took the road to the hills, trudging along in the sun's glare.

The Country Cottage

The road began to wind up a stony valley. Round a corner they came to a cottage, surrounded by fig and olive trees. It was very small, a log hut, with thatched roof, and a pillared porch to catch the cool of the evening. A few hens scratched around the step. In the garden were a grey goose and an old man watering rows of lettuces. "Good day, sirs," called the old man as they came up. "Good day to you, old man," said Zeus. "Can you give us something to quench our thirst? The dust on the road is choking us." "Come in, and welcome," said the old man. "All strangers are welcome, for they come in the name of Zeus. Philemon is my name and I live here with Baucis my wife. Baucis! Here are two travellers asking for something to drink." An old woman, black-shawled, her face a smiling map of wrinkles, came to meet them in the doorway. "You are welcome, strangers," she said. "Bend your heads as you come in. The door is very low for two gentlemen as tall as yourselves."

They groped their way into the hut, hardly able to see, after the dazzle of sunshine outside. Philemon guided them to a bench by the door, over which Baucis spread a cloth of homespun wool, threadbare but very clean. The gods sat down, stretching their tired legs with sighs of pleasure. Meanwhile Baucis was blowing up the wood fire and setting an iron pot to boil, and Philemon brought in firewood and fresh herbs from the garden. "You will eat with us, of course," he said, as proud in his poor hut as any chieftain in a high hall. "Baucis will bring you warm water to wash, for I see you are tired and dusty from your journey." One could see it made no difference in that house whether you asked for master or servant. The old people were both, and they had learnt to live happily with poverty. Philemon unhooked a beechwood trough from its peg on the wall. Baucis poured in a cauldron of steaming water, which she cooled with buckets from the well.

While the two gods splashed gratefully in the clear spring water, the old man and woman went about their household tasks. First Baucis scrubbed the stripped pine table, already white from a lifetime's scouring, and rubbed it down with fresh-scented mint. Then she set it out in the porch, where trellised vines hung down in a curtain of green. The table legs were unsteady, so she propped it on an old tile. Philemon heaped up a couch of straw, and threw over it a hand-woven rug, soft and faded as sunset's end. This they kept for great occasions. He took a haymaker's fork and unhooked the flitch of bacon from the blackened rafters under the roof. Deftly he cut off a piece, which Baucis put in the pot, with a clove of garlic and sprigs of thyme, mint and parsley. By the time the two gods had finished bathing, a tempting smell of boiled bacon was rising from the pot. Baucis had set the table with her trembling old hands and now beckoned them to sit down.

The table was spread with salad, wild berries and lettuce, black olives, scarlet radishes and an earthenware bowl of eggs, slowly baked on the embers of the fire. "I am sure the gods on Mount Olympus enjoy no better feast," cried young Hermes. The father of the gods frowned at him severely. "Our guests are welcome," said the old man with dignity, and filled their wooden drinking bowls with rough, home-made wine. When the bacon was set before them the two gods soon finished it up, and sent back their beechwood platters for figs and pomegranates, apples, nuts, and honey in the comb.

Above all, there was cheerful company in that rough cottage as the old couple chatted with their guests. Philemon told how he had run away with Baucis from her father's house when she was a girl, as is still the custom at weddings in hill villages. He told how they worked together on their little farm. In November he ploughed, while she walked after, sowing beans or barley out of her apron. In May he harvested with his curved sickle, and she helped him to trample the grain on the threshing floor. At harvest, like countryfolk everywhere, they hid a corn dolly, and brought it out next spring like Persephone, bearing green shoots of the new year's crop. In summer they hoed and watered their vegetable patch, and in September picked the grapes to make their wine. Baucis baked barley loaves and tended her bees. In winter she set up her loom and wove woollen cloaks against the bite of mountain air. "She's a good farmer's wife," said the old man proudly.

Pausing in his talk, Philemon took up the wineskin to refill their bowls. But his hand stopped in mid air and a great fear seized his heart, for the skin, which had been half empty, was full again, full of a dark, rich wine, scented with honey, a god-like wine, never tasted in that poor cottage before. Then Philemon and Baucis knew that their unknown guests were immortals, and together they fell on their knees to plead forgiveness for the simple welcome which was all they could offer. They knew the gods bring bitter misfortune on those who are fated to displease them. They remembered stories from their childhood: a boy changed to a lizard, a girl into a spider, a party of peasants condemned to be frogs, and they trembled.

Then a thought struck them both and together they ran to catch the grey goose and offer it as a sacrifice to appease the gods. But the goose had no mind to die so soon. It ran, hissing and flapping its wings, to take shelter under the cloak of Zeus himself. "Let the creature live," said Zeus. "We are gods and mean to punish this unfriendly countryside as it deserves, but you shall escape. Follow me to the top of your mountain."

In awed silence the couple set out on the steep path behind the strangers. It seemed to old, bent Baucis, that she had never climbed the steep rocks so swiftly or easily, not even when she first came to the cottage as a fresh young bride. "Turn and look down on the valley," commanded Zeus, when they stood on the peak. They turned and saw below them a vast silver lake. Little waves were lapping the mountain side and the city of Tyana was drowned deep under the flood. A lonely heron wheeled over the market place and fish swam through the streets where the gods had asked in vain for shelter.

The old people looked for their cottage, fearful and sad at heart, for they expected to see the waves cover its roof. But there, by the lake shore, before their eyes, the porch soared upwards on lofty pillars of marble, the mud walls dissolved into airy colonnades, and the dusty thatch began to shine like beaten gold. Then Zeus spoke, his deep voice rolling like thunder around the mountain tops. "This cottage shall be a temple in my honour, and you, good old man and woman, shall be priest and priestess there. When old age makes your steps slow, and your hands too feeble to harvest the corn and the olive, you shall not lose the home you have loved, but live there in peace and honour to the end of your days. Tell me what you most desire in the world and I will give it to you, for I am Zeus the Thunderer, ruler of gods and men."

Philemon and Baucis whispered together for a moment and the husband spoke for both. "Oh great Zeus, we have lived so long in peace and love together that we dread the hour of parting. Let me never see the tomb of my wife, nor let her weep by my grave, but let us die, we beg you, in the same hour." It was as they had asked. One day, as the two old guardians stood before the steps of the temple, Philemon saw branches and leaves spring from the arms of his wife, and her long hair turn green as willow twigs. "Farewell, Philemon," she cried, as branches covered her face. "Farewell Baucis, my dear one," he cried as bark closed over his own lips. There by the lake a willow tree and an oak grow side by side, swaying with every breath of wind. They say you may hear the leaves still whispering, "Farewell: farewell."

The Spirits of Wild Places

Before the first man lived, earth made the nymphs, whose name means "young brides". In their lovely shapes live the spirits of wild places. They eat the immortal food of the gods, but they have no wish to live in the sky's golden palace, for they love the fern-scented hollows of earth. The land of Greece is thirsty. Heat dances on the stones in dry river beds, splits the figs where they hang from the tree and burns the summer hillsides brown. Yet where the nymphs live the woods are shadowy and quiet. The tree-nymph lays a cool finger to her lips, guarding the travellers rest; the nymph of the spring gives him clear water so that he may drink and bathe.

These girls of the lovely locks are forever young, forever beautiful. Pan pipes to them when evening comes; the goat-legged satyrs join their woodland games. The nymphs love handsome mortals, possessing them with a divine vision of nature. Yet if men try to seize them, chasing the empty air with hopes they cannot catch, the nymphs flee away.

So it will always be with mortals and wild places. Once possessed they are lost. The songs and tales of the nymphs are past counting. Here are two, among many.

The first is the tale of Arethusa, a nymph who served Artemis and followed in her train. One evening Arethusa returned from hunting, breathless and weary. She came to a stream, flowing cold and clear, so clear she could see to count the shining pebbles in its bed. The bank sloped gently to the water's edge and willows made a green tent around her. Arethusa stepped in, feeling the coldness of melted mountain snow around her ankles, fresh and tingling. Quickly she unfastened her girdle, hung her tunic on a branch and dived naked into the deep water. The river flowed smooth and green around her, stroking her body with long ripples of cold. The nymph swam fearlessly, kicking up fountains of bright spray.

Suddenly she heard or felt a murmuring in the depths of the water. Like a wild creature sensing danger, she leapt out on the far bank, just as the river god rose from his bed and stretched out dripping arms to seize her. The naked nymph ran and the god pressed fiercely after her, as a hawk chases its prey down the streams of the wind. "Arethusa!" he shouted, harsh as the rattle of stones in a torrent. "Why are you running away? Come back! Come back!" She ran on, over windy headlands, through dark woods, over rocks and crags, leaping the lip of the waterfall, her wet hair streaming in her wake. She was fast, but the god was stronger.

They came to the shore of the western sea. Arethusa saw his long shadow stretch out to cover her, heard his thundering footsteps, felt the cold breath of his spray in her hair. "Save me, hide me, great goddess!" she cried in terror. At this prayer, Artemis sent a cloud from the silent snows and cast it round her follower like a cloak. But the river god was not deceived. He could not see the girl but no footprints led away from the place and he knew she must be there. He circled round and round her. You may see the windings of his river to this day. Twice he called her name, in his harsh torrent's voice, twice he stretched out rivulets which almost touched her as she stood shuddering on the cliff.

Then Arethusa wept in despair. Tears flowed from her eyes, spray from her hair. Pools of clear water formed round her feet. Artemis loudly called to her brother, the sea, the waves divided and Arethusa plunged into the depths. On she flowed,

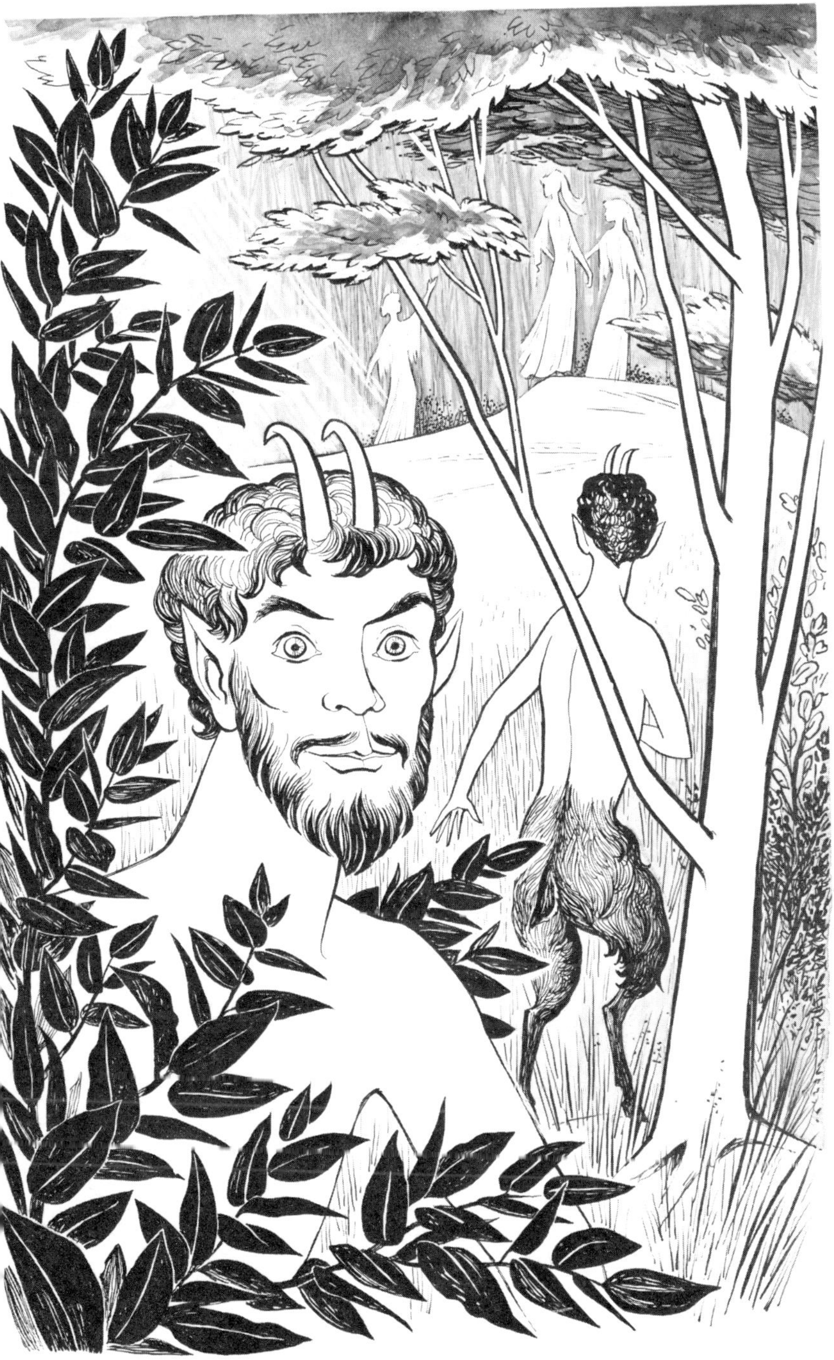

a current so swift she has given her name to many sailing ships. She flowed through sea-caverns, where Ocean's daughters sit on shell thrones, through coral forests and rays of shimmering light. Faster than swordfish, faster than dolphin, she flowed towards Sicily. Yet all the time the river god rushed after, in a torrent of stones and silt that stained the green sea brown far out from land. Still he surged on, longing to mingle himself in the waters he loved.

Swift Arethusa at last came to Sicily, to the island of Ortygia in the harbour of Syracuse. There she surfaced as a spring, which still bubbles fresh and clear from the rock. In her stone fountain trout and carp glide through the water; her tall reeds sway and whisper in the wind. Nearby on the shore her lover, the river, flows. Fishermen beach their boats and clean their catch in his waters. Fear and desire are over for these lovers now, since they share the same nature. Both flow quietly and, in the coolness of their breath, wild mimosa brushes the traveller's hand.

The second is a grimmer tale, for wild creatures of the open air revenge themselves on despoiling men. Nymphs lived as easily in the cold rains of autumn and the shrieking winter wind as in summer's golden days, and they were more powerful than any mortal. An old rhyme reckoned their age. "Nine human spans lives the rook, a stag as long as four rooks, a raven as long as three stags, a palm as long as nine ravens, and as long as ten palms live the nymphs of the lovely locks." None lived longer than the dryads, nymphs of the great oak trees.

Greatest of all was the nymph of Demeter's grove in Thessaly. This sacred oak had grown for longer than man's memory, overshadowing the other trees of the wood, its leafy boughs a city of birds. Its spreading branches were hung with wreaths and garlands left by mortals who had prayed to the goddess there. Round its huge trunk the nymphs joined hands and danced, singing their secret songs. Demeter, mother of harvests, spread her blessing over her worshippers in its green shade, granting them joy in their crops and children. Happy are those who honour her, for she feeds all living creatures, on land or sea or flying in the air, from her rich store.

Yet in Thessaly there was a lord who wanted oak logs to build a hall for feasting. He was a man who scorned the gods. In an evil hour he took an axe and went with his servants to Demeter's tree. "Cut down this tree," he commanded, but even the slaves hung back in dread. "I say it shall be felled!" shouted the blustering fool. "Yes, if it were the goddess herself, not just her tree, I would bring it to the ground!" Swinging the heavy axe with both hands, he brought it crashing down upon the trunk. The oak tree trembled, like the living creature it was. Colour fled from its leaves and acorns, while the heavy boughs writhed like arms. He dragged out the axe. The tree's lifeblood flowed from the gash in the bark like a slaughtered beast. The servants stood in mute horror. "Stop before it is too late!" cried one bolder than the rest. For answer his master turned and swung the axe on him. Then he fell on the tree like a madman, driven by fate, hacking it with blow after blow, till the sound of the axe rang through the echoing grove defiling the beauty that other men had gazed at.

Suddenly a voice spoke from the heart of the tree. "I am the nymph of the oak," it whispered, through all its rustling leaves. "I live within this tree and the Mother Goddess loves me. Build yourself a banqueting hall, cruel man, for you will need one. This I warn you with my dying breath." The murmur of the branches faded under the cruel blows of the axe. Then the man called for ropes, and bound the noble trunk, shouting to his servants to haul on the slack. The death agony of the great tree was dreadful to watch. It groaned and shuddered through all its thousand branches, then came crashing to the ground. A cry went up from the wood, a rustling of leaves as the other dryads tossed their branches and swayed in grief for their dead sister. They threw off their lovely leaves and bright berries in mourning and begged Demeter, bareheaded, to punish the murderer.

The vain and foolish man built a high hall from the oak logs. Sadly they did forced labour in a stranger's house like slaves, while their own home lay desolate. Then he invited his friends to a banquet. But by Demeter's command the nymphs went to a stony field, where hollow-eyed Hunger lived, tearing up the weeds with her nails and teeth, and invited her to the feast. Hunger came. She flung her skeleton arms round the lord of the hall, breathing into his lips and spreading famine through his body.

He sat at his table, laden with all the good things Demeter gives to her children: smoking dishes of roast meat, silvery fish, crusted bread and gleaming fruit. He gulped the whole feast down, but all his champing jaws and greedy gullet swallowed was thin air. He shouted for more and still more banquets to satisfy his craving, enough to feed an army, a city, a whole nation; his family fortune was all spent on food and he was ruined. Yet still hunger gnawed and raged within his body, till the people said his stomach must be a bottomless pit, for everything vanished into it. At last hunger ate him up entirely and with his death the nymph of the oak tree was avenged. So sure death waits for those who defile nature. Yet earth's wild places give delight to those who honour the lovely nymphs of mountain, wood and stream.

The Tellers of Tales

ONE place is joyous beyond all others. Here Pegasus, the winged horse, stamped his hoof and from his footprint a clear fountain flowed. Here among cool groves and meadows of starry petals the Muses were born. These lovely sisters were the daughters of Memory, herself a daughter of the sky that overarches all. They knew all things that were past, all music, all dancing, all stories that ever were told.

Each had treasures in her keeping and their names were a song: she of the fair voice, she of the double flute, she with the scroll of great deeds, she with the starry globe, dark she and fair she with the masks of tragedy and comedy, she who sings of love, she who delights to dance and she of the many songs. No greater joy has ever been on earth, they say, than to hear the Muses singing with garlands in their hair. All men adored them with temple-offerings and festivals of music. Yet they chose to live simply beside their spring, sharing their treasure with mortals in the pure shape of water.

For the violet-crowned sisters allowed mortal men and women to drink at their spring, and whoever drank there was inspired. Ever after they delighted to make lovely things from the Muses' store. Such were the tellers of tales. Theirs was a high destiny, and their fame flew far across earth and sea. Often they were poor, yet many were richer because of them. The circling hours at work brought them contentment. They found the delight that each day brings and came to their fated end in calm of mind, leaving good things behind them. They were happy men and women, guarding with stylus and wax tablet the treasures of memory. Ancient beauty falls asleep and men forget it if no one tells of it, but gods and men live again in the words of the Muses' servants. Because of them these tales are still told.

THRACE
MACEDONIA
Mt.Olympus
EPIRUS
LEMNOS
THESSALY
AEGEAN
SEA
EUBOEA
AETOLIA
Mt.Parnassus
ITHACA
Calydon
Delphi
Mt.Helion
Thebes
ATTICA
Eleusis
Athens
ACHAIA
ANDR
Corinth
Elis
IONIAN
SEA
Mycenae
ARGOLIS
ARCADIA
Argos
Troezen
PELOPONNESUS
Sparta
SERIPHOS
Pylos
LACONIA
CYTHERA
MEDITERRANEAN
SEA
MILES
0
20
40
60
80
100
0
40
80
120
160
KILOMETRES
Knos